ON BEING BLACKFELLA'S YOUNG FELLA

IS BEING ABORIGINAL ENOUGH?

GLENN LOUGHREY

Published in Australia by
Coventry Press
33 Scoresby Road
Bayswater Vic. 3153
Australia

ISBN 9781922589286

Copyright © Glenn Loughrey 2020

All rights reserved. Other than for the purposes and subject to the conditions prescribed under the *Copyright Act*, no part of this publication may be reproduced, stored in a retrieval system, or transmitted in any form or by any means, electronic, mechanical, photocopying, recording or otherwise, without the prior permission of the publisher.

Cataloguing-in-Publication entry is available from the National Library of Australia http://catalogue.nla.gov.au/.

Cover design by Ian James - www.jgd.com.au
Cover photograph by David Merrylees
Text design by Megan Low (Film Shot Graphics FSG)
Typeset in Minion Pro

Printed in Australia

CONTENTS

Acknowledgment of Country 5
Dedication 6
Forewords 7
Introduction 11
Aboriginal Spirituality 21
A Little Bit of History 31
In the Good Old Days 39
On Being Aboriginal 49
This Ground, She's My Mother 59
    I am my country 62
    The land owns us 68
    Self-determination 70
Wiradjuri Dreaming 73
Repository of Sacred Texts 81
    Kinship 83
    Lore/Law 87
    Language 90
    Ceremony/Rituals/Story 92
The Rocks Speak 95
Universe as Country 103
    The universe to the particular; the particular
    to the universe. 108
Living the Change 115
    Questions 118
    So what would that look like? 120

Patterns Everywhere..............................123
Whin-nga-rra....................................131
All in the Sky 137
An Intricate Web of Inter-Being-Ness 143
In Conclusion...................................149
References......................................156

ACKNOWLEDGMENT OF COUNTRY

> *I acknowledge the sovereign land giving birth to and providing abundantly for the peoples of the Kulin nations on which I now live. I recognise their elder's past, present and future. I give thanks for their generosity in allowing me to live, work, write and speak from this place.*
> *I also acknowledge that this land was stolen and those who stole it have no intentions of giving it back any time soon.*

Notice that I acknowledged country and not people. The first thing an indigenous person asks you is where you are from?[1] The answer is your country. Why? Because it establishes your identity, from where you gain the sovereignty embedded in your body - my body, my country. It identifies the vessel containing you and whom you carry in your body - your Aboriginality, identifying you as a citizen of the universe.

I acknowledge the history of our country. The land has been stolen and will not be returned. We are where we are in this country's history because of the myth of settlement of empty land.[2] No treaty and no accommodation of the sovereignty of the many custodian nations have been negotiated. The sovereignty of the land has not been ceded. We are living in our country under the occupation of a colonial government.

---

1   Behrendt, Larissa; *Decolonising Research: Indigenous Story Work as Methodology*, Edited by Jo-Ann Archibald Q'umQ'umXilem, Jenny Bol Jun Lee-Morgan, Jason De Santolo, Zed Books Pty, Ltd, 2019, p. 176.
2   Terra Nullius and the Doctrine of Discovery

DEDICATION

I dedicate this book to the following:

- To my father, grandmother and great-grandfather, who were never told they were enough; and my mother who nurtured us through it all.

- To my wife Gaye, our daughter Katrina and Jemma, the English Springer Spaniel, who supported me in this journey.

- To the congregation of St Oswald's, Glen Iris, for their willingness to explore our interlocked history.

FOREWORDS

The word spirituality is in vogue at the present time. It can often be thought of as other worldly and esoteric practices, or the preserve of people who dress differently to others and have an air of mystique. It is often seen as a commodity that can be bought, or learnt, at meditational retreats in 'glamped' up bush settings, and there are many who are willing to pay. In our consumer, and time poor world, spirituality can be purchased and time minimised with the right accoutrements, candles, incense, and clothing. Colourful and mystical looking books with wise and pithy sayings abound. Pack all this in your backpack and you are on the spiritual road.

I sound disdainful, but there is truth in this. We are time poor and relatively wealthy, and consumerism has taught us that if want it, all we need to do is buy it. There is, of course, a positive in this consumer spirituality. People are looking for deeper things that a consumer market cannot really provide. Many want to be in touch with their spirit and with a greater force they sense hovering over this creation. They are looking for meaning, and the consumer path before them provides many people with an attractive option.

In this quest for spiritual meaning, Indigenous spirituality seems like a very attractive option. It seems mystical and otherworldly, haunting even, and somehow will give us all the answers we need for a 21st century world. The interest in Aboriginal Spirituality is growing in Australia as many people think that the experience of Aboriginal people has the answers they need, except they will leave behind the nasty historical bits to do with massacres and genocide. People are searching for an Australian identity, and they reckon that Aboriginal people just might provide the answer.

Glenn Loughrey's work takes us down a different path; a different journey. Spirituality is not something readily learnt. It has to with identity and place. It is no flight to fancy from reality, but a living within our own skin, on our country, within our history; a sense of self in the community of others found in deep places. Glenn invites us to listen deeply. It is his story he shares. His struggles. His insights. I might part company with Glenn on a few things, especially his view on the place of Christianity in the context of Aboriginal spirituality, but it is his story, not mine; yet, at the same time, it is both of ours seen through the same refracted lens of contemporary Aboriginal experience.

Glenn is to be commended for this work of deep reflection. He invites the reader to listen deeply, and, in listening deeply, the reader will find their own place; their own 'songlines'. Spirituality is not bought or taught, but lived and shared. Glenn does this well. Glenn's work is one of integrity and bravery as he wrestles publicly with his identity and Christian faith in the context of being an Anglican priest. Perhaps, the lesson learnt from this book is that Aboriginal spirituality is not to be appropriated. It is our story and journey as Aboriginal people. It belongs to us. What Glenn has done for many is point the direction for a journey of self-discovery. I thank him for his story and explorations; I have learnt deeply from them.

> We shall not cease from exploration
> And the end of all our exploring

Forewords

Will be to arrive where we started
And know the place for the first time.

T. S. Eliot – Little Gidding

> The Rt Rev'd Chris McLeod
> National Aboriginal Bishop
> Anglican Church of Australia

***

Glenn Loughrey writes honestly and accurately. His language is strong, informed, troubled; and not far from the surface we see his vulnerability. He tells us that he has been living into his Aboriginality since in his 40s and his faithful pursuit of this truth makes his latest book a compelling read.

Established in his identity as an Anglican priest, truth-seeking now requires him to question everything about this: atonement theologies; dualism; the Church as a social control agent for colonial governments, various related duplicities.

I was left looking forward to a conversation with Glenn about Jesus and the power of love (as compared to the love of power). This conversation would be about - as Glenn writes – 'finding a religion suitable to Australia and all who live here'.

We see glimpses in Glenn's writing of what this 'suitable religion' might be. A religion of being, where spirituality is not a separated matter from how we listen to all creation in 'the interconnectedness of life on the land and how' - as Glenn learned from his father in childhood at Ulan - 'every decision had consequences, was connected, made a pattern and if you did this, then you would need to do that'. In making his truth-seeking vivid for us, Glenn is also providing timely wisdom as we respond to the reality of climate change.

Whilst it is urgent that we reduce greenhouse gas emissions as fast as possible, Glenn cautions that there is no quick fix to understanding the interdependence of being. 'I am through you, so I' includes our burnt earth from summers fires; the echidna and wallaby, the waterways and the fish amidst plastic in the ocean.

As Glenn writes: 'You cannot just go out after forty minutes of workshop and hear the ancestors and, come to think of it, our world, only responds to a respectful and reciprocal relationship; and, without that, what we may listen to is only our desires echoing back to us'. We need better than that. Australia needs healing, at many levels.

By writing with such honesty and knowledge, Glenn is a blessed and loveable guide for the days ahead.

The Rt Rev'd Philip Huggins
Regional bishop, Diocese of Melbourne
Anglican Church of Australia

INTRODUCTION

When I decided to write a book on Aboriginal[3] spirituality, I had a specific goal in mind: to write about our spirituality and how it deserved its place in the religious landscape of Australia.

I had only recently dialogued with John Bell,[4] a Celtic religious songwriter, and had found it disturbing. We were to talk about the intersection of Aboriginal and Celtic spirituality. My intention then was to engage with, not Celtic or Aboriginal Christianity, but the foundational roots of spirituality in both our traditions. It didn't go as I intended. John was focused almost entirely on Celtic Christianity and not where I wanted us to be.

My initial reaction was to be both disappointed and afraid. Disappointed that what I had so wanted to happen did not – a revelation, perhaps, of the similarities in our foundational stories. Fearful, because I did not wish what I perceived to have happened in Scotland – the eradication of a way of being and seeing – replaced by a particular type of religious faith – Christianity.

I was doubly afraid as this raised conflict within me as both an Aboriginal person and a Christian priest. What would happen to my vocation if I took this seriously and opted for being the first over the second? Can they co-exist, or are they mutually exclusive?

---

3 In this text, I will use a range of words to describe the original people, including Aboriginal, Indigenous, First Nations People, and my own mob's name Wiradjuri.

4 En.wikipedia.org. (2019). *John L. Bell*. [online] Available at: https://en.wikipedia.org/wiki/John L. Bell [Accessed 12 Sep. 2019].

I am aware that many do hold them together – perhaps in tension – but together. I was not confident I could do the same. This has been a growing concern for me since becoming a priest in 2009. Back then, it seemed the logical thing to do. Yes, I was Aboriginal, but Christianity was the only spirituality I had known, outwardly at least, since a child. Because of our family's story (a little too complicated to record here), we were white Australians, a little dusty and sunburnt in places, but white nevertheless.

Growing up on the farm outside Ulan,[5] I learned much about the land from my father. He seemed to understand its every move, walked across it daily, listened to the birds, animals, trees, and rocks, and explained patiently what it all meant. In short, if you listen carefully, you will hear, and you will know what to do. Here was my first interaction with deep thinking, whin-nga-rra[6], a critical indigenous practice informing pattern thinking and an anticipatory world-view.

I was living on top of the Great Dividing Range. It seemed actually to divide the east from the west. From the top, water ran both ways, rivers ran differently on one side to how they ran on the other, and we could see both ways. Maybe this was a metaphor for how I grew up, unconsciously seeing both ways. I didn't know it then, but it is not a Divide at all. It is a north-south-north song line connecting people down the east coast of Australia. Maybe this is another metaphor of being sung into being – to sing others

---

5 En.wikipedia.org. (2019). *Ulan, New South Wales*. [online] Available at: https://en.wikipedia.org/wiki/Ulan, New South Wales [Accessed 12 Sep, 2019].
6 RegenR8. (2019). *Wiradjuri Dictionary - RegenR8*. [online] Available at: https://regenr8.org/language-revitalisation/apps/wiradjuri-dictionary/ [Accessed 12 Sep. 2019].

Introduction

into being – through connection and story (it wouldn't be *my* actual singing skills that would do it, though!)

I have vivid memories of walking back and forth across the land as a child. Over two thousand, five hundred acres is a big back yard, and it held many mysteries and wild things to get to know and explore. Sitting in the big Moreton Bay fig tree on the ridge of the range and watching kangaroos (wambuwuny), wallabies (gundhirrwa), and wallaroos (walaru) come out at dusk to feed on the paddocks laid out before me. Listening to crows (waagan), cockatoos (wayimaa), galahs (gilaa), kookaburras (guguburra), magpies (garru), currawongs (wuyung) and more calling back and forth to each other. The occasional fox[7] would appear, along with the ubiquitous rabbit. It was my menagerie where I whiled away many hours just watching.

Walking my country and listening to it, I heard, deep down within me, the resonance of belonging and being one with it, which has never gone away. Like my father, I cried every time I went past the old place now cut up into twenty-five-acre blocks, and all my cousins[8] have disappeared from view, forced off the land we shared with them.

Driving past the burgeoning Ulan, Wilpinjong, and Moolarben coal mines consuming my grandmother's and my father's childhood home and much of the sacred sites and artefacts of people long since eradicated is traumatic. Looking across Byer's[9] paddock toward the now empty riverbed (it was

---

7   There is no word in our language for fox as these are not native animals.
8   'All my cousins' refers to all created beings (fauna and flora) and the earth we share this world with, as citizens of the universe.
9   The old Byer's family farm was on the banks of the Goulburn River outside Ulan.

unsuccessfully moved and still doesn't run), I remember the silver eels (galin-dulin) we used to catch there when they were running. What a joyous occasion now consigned to a fading memory, a victim of economic progress.

The sandstone rocks and caverns above the creek across from Grandma's house where we used to play, the river itself where we swam as little kids and the old gum tree under which I caught a six-foot goanna (gugaa) in a rabbit trap are all gone. As gugaa is a tribal totem, we couldn't kill him, so imagine a ten or eleven-year-old using a very long stick to try and loosen the rabbit (wadha-gung) trap so he could get out, and when he did, making sure he didn't mistake you for a tree and so run up and sat on your head. (I think my Uncle Pud was pulling my leg with the last bit!)

Only three sacred sites remain in the Ulan area. Two are readily accessible – the Hands on the Rocks and the Drip or dripping wall. The other, the Baby Foot Cave, is on land 'owned' by the mine and not accessible to non-mine personnel. Restoration of the Hands on the Rocks allows gabaas (white men or strangers)[10] to look at the hands close up from walkways and platforms running across the ceremonial spaces. Here those who owned the Hands had sat, dialogued, and agreed, placing their hands on the rocks, affirming their presence and agreement. In ancient times, this space occupied the edge of several surrounding countries[11] and was, in some ways, a liminal or safe space for inter-tribal discussions. The idea of building platforms for tourists to view the sacred Hands sits uncomfortably with me.

---

10   Wiradjuri Dictionary
11   Wiradjuri, Kamilaroi, Geagel, Wonnarua.

Introduction

The Dripping Wall – or as the locals know it, The Drip – is on the Goulburn River just a stone's throw from the Hands on the Rock. Here the water drips down the sandstone wall into the river below where it makes a full pool surrounded by large rocks. It is sacred as it was a place where women from the surrounding tribes came to give birth. It was a special women's place, and we were never allowed to swim in it. My father would always stand a little way off.

It played a cameo in my childhood. My father came home from work on a Monday evening. He was working in a slate or white clay mine where it is possible that those who made the hand paintings got the white clay used in making the handprints.[12]

Somehow he and his best friend learned of some shenanigans that had occurred at the Drip over the weekend. "Bloody hippies" (Dad's words when he came home) had been wandering around the site naked while drawing on the sandstone rocks nearby. Dad was livid and went looking for the interlopers. He did not go empty-handed but with a loaded gun, ready to deal with those who had interfered with the sacred space. They didn't find them, fortunately, as I could have found fame as the son of the man who shot Brett Whitely.

At the release of the movie about Brett's life,[13] I spoke to Wendy, his wife, who was surprised that Brett's drawings remain because there was one angry man on the rampage whom they assumed would have destroyed any evidence of the pictures.[14]

---

12 https://www.dpi.nsw.gov.au/__data/assets/pdf_file/0008/109817/mining-by-aborigines.pdf
13 Whiteley. (2019). *Whiteley*. [online] Available at: https://whiteleythefilm.com.au/ [Accessed 12 Sep. 2019].
14 Meacham, S. (2019). *Saga of nude Brett Whiteley's cave painting*. [online]

Anger sat just below the surface for my father. It was never far away. Outwardly, he was friendly and personable; inwardly, it seems to me, he was angry at the hand life dealt him and always seeking to find acceptance. As a young man who went shearing, his anger saw release via the contract shearers lifestyle where drinking and fighting were recreational activities. I suspect these kept the lid on things at one level and allowed it to lift just a little at the same time.

Later, as a married man and father, the fighting as an outlet faded, although I do remember a dance at Uarbry[15] where the men stayed outside drinking beer brought in the boots of cars and engaged in organised bouts. After it was over, they came and danced the night away with their partners, as if nothing had happened.

Life changed drastically for us when my parents had a dream; they wanted a farm and, conveniently, the local Post Office and farm came on the market. They did a small business plan and made an appointment with a regional bank manager Dad knew. We all dressed in our Sunday best; Dad in a suit and tie and Mum wore the best hat she had made. We set off the twenty miles to town with high hopes.

Now my father was always known as Blackfella or Darkie. I was and remain Young Blackfella, Blackfella's Young Fella, or Young Darkie. I thought it was because my father worked outside and was suntanned and weather-beaten. That morning, I was to find out something that changed my life.

The Sydney Morning Herald. Available at: https://www.smh.com.au/entertainment/art-and-design/saga-of-nude-brett-whiteleys-cave-painting-20090312-gdteuo.html [Accessed 12 Sep. 2019].
15 Uarbry is a small hamlet between Duneedoo and Coolah in NSW.

Introduction

On arrival, the staff ushered us into the manager's office. There were some toys to play with, and my brother and I sat quietly in the corner. We knew the rules and how important this was. Mum and Dad outlined their plans, and when they finished, all went quiet, waiting for the answer. They were hopeful because the two men played cricket together, so they knew each other.

'No, we don't lend to people like you, Blackfella.'

As the manager carefully explained the decision, our lives changed. Alcohol and violence became the only way my father could deal with disappointment, creating significant trauma for Mum and me as the oldest son until he stopped drinking in his mid-fifties. While the alcohol and violence disappeared, his anger remained. His anger stemmed from his perception of not being accepted and included in the Whiteman's world.

Another time, my father was offered an incentive by the farmer he worked for, promising a financial share of the crop if he was able to secure a specific yield in the harvest. He worked hard to ensure that this was the best-prepared paddock in which to sow wheat. When harvested, it not only achieved the agreed yield but posted a record for the local area. He could not wait for the 'bonus' at Christmas time to pick up his share of the profit. Instead, when he came home, all he had received was a blue esky.[16] He would say, 'That's the most expensive esky in Australia'.

When my father walked away from the job on the farm, we moved to town. Somewhere in my schooling, I began to understand I was not the same as those around me, noticing people treated me differently. I experienced bullying at school,

---

16 A generic name for a portable cooler.

but then many did. It was the casual comments coming from classmates and parents, which began to awaken that perception of difference.

In a spat with a schoolmate, I was called 'the son of a drunk bush black'. Another time, I was part of a group in a local club for a meeting of Rotary. I was in the school Interact club. After the meal, I got up and went to the toilet. As I was coming back, I heard one of the fathers – a man my father had done a lot of business with – say, 'You can be friends with him but just remember where he comes from and who he is'.

I remember an English class where we were discussing the book *The Chant of Jimmy Blacksmith*.[17] I mentioned that my great-grandfather had watched them as they travelled past the house. They waved at each other. The class all laughed. It wasn't until much later I found out why. It appears from my research that we are intricately connected to Jimmy Governor with the distinct possibility that Grandma was his child and Roy Governor, the last Aboriginal bushranger, was her step-brother. As noted elsewhere, there was no record of a father; and her mother's details are scant.

It seemed that everyone knew this story except me.

The difference became a part of my life, and I discovered no matter how good I was, I was never good enough. Even though I had the same sporting and academic skills as most in my year level, I was always the outsider. And outsider I have stayed. There is much more to this story, but that will have to wait for another day.

---

17   Keneally, Thomas. *The Chant of Jimmie Blacksmith,* Sydney: Angus and Robertson 1972.

Introduction

Suffice to say, I sought ways to be a part of society; and being a Christian and an Anglican Priest seemed as good as any. Being an Anglican priest is the whitest thing a blackfella could do! If you are going to assimilate, you most well be in an organisation with the Queen as the head! My mum was delighted.

I wasn't sure. Not only was the Queen the head but those who had exterminated the local tribal people in just fifty years were primarily Anglican. They gave the ground and funded the local church where I had served as an altar boy in my teens. Is it appropriate for me to be one among those who purposely practised genocide, replaced our Aboriginality with Christianity, and strove to make us white? In the right sunlight, you could say it nearly worked on me!

My father would say, 'That man (insert name) is a white man', meaning he was a good man. I grew up hearing only white was good. Black was not.

That is where I am now, and what follows is a journey into a greater understanding of Aboriginality as a way of being human in this space we call Australia. There is no such thing as Aboriginal spirituality, only Aboriginality, and I hope to show why as you read on.

ABORIGINAL SPIRITUALITY

I awoke in the middle of the night. The sky was dark. The air was still, and not a creature stirred. Dread had overcome me, and I lay there, as still as the night, with just the breathing of my dog Jemma punctuating the silence.

Not an unusual circumstance for me, especially since I began to work through what it means to be an Aboriginal or Indigenous or a First Nations Person or Wiradjuri, depending on how you see it. This is always a work in progress and never a linear pathway as there is no such thing as a straight line in Aboriginal thinking. It is a circular-like movement; one moment, you are forging ahead, and the next, you are back, snakelike, eating your tail. At that moment, you find yourself shedding your skin in recognition of a new insight, replacing what you had previously thought, spoken or written.

This journey is a journey of inconsistency. What I say today, illumined by new insights, may be very different from what I said yesterday. This is what happened in the dark of the night. It occurred to me that perhaps, just perhaps, that there is no such category as Aboriginal spirituality. What if this category was and is a colonised term used to identify something mysterious to settlers?

What does it mean to be Aboriginal? What are Aboriginal ways of seeing, and how do we label and place them alongside something familiar in our context? What if being Aboriginal is enough, without the need to add the category 'spirituality' to the word?

Western culture, thanks to the Greeks, majors on dualities, in the form of either-or, this or that, same-different, spiritual-material, and more. Categories are essential for identifying what is or is not. We definitively use them; in other words, if it is this, it cannot be that. There is no spiritual within the material. Rocks are physical phenomena, not spiritual in life. They can be picked up, put down, cut open, crushed, analysed, and named. They are not, in the Western mind, sentient beings and, therefore, cannot be spiritual.

In traditional western religions, spiritual takes on a distinct sense. It is the evidence of faith as a particular form of understanding. It is exclusive to those who correctly practise religion. Not all people are spiritual; only those who conform to a specific definition and idea of what it means to be people of faith are spiritual. It is not universal, and it is not a normalised way of being human.

Being spiritual is a choice. You decide to be so and then adapt your life around the concept you understand and practise. You practise your spirituality, perhaps initially as an adjunct to your previously regular life, before it begins to define you, and you disappear into it as a way of being. It becomes you, and you become it.

Being spiritual takes on specific practices and rituals you use to confirm your spirituality and being – meditation, yoga, prayer, worship, crystals, gratitude, veganism, and more. These become

Aboriginal Spirituality

signposts of who you are and are necessary to maintain your place in the world. They become embedded as non-negotiable.

One of the ways colonisation replaces indigenous culture is by appropriating concepts and ideas and transforming them into accepted practice. Deep thinking is a case in point. What is a form of seeing and being for Aboriginal people becomes an individualistic religious practice and equated with prayer, meditation, mindfulness, health, and more.

It is none of these in essence or practice. It comes as part of the package in your skin when you are born under a tree, and you grow into it as you mature and travel through your life. It is not about self but all selves you are connected with by simply being. It is how you listen, hear and think. In Wiradjuri, it is whin-nga-grra,[18] and it sits in the gut of all.

What woke me up was the realisation that, thanks to Tyson Yunkaporta, spiritual is not an Aboriginal category. I guess I knew that already. I have read all the critical books and battled with the growing awareness that I am innately a spiritual being, and it ties directly to my Aboriginality. How I see others and how I resonate with country, its presence in my body, affirms that I experience a deep one-ness or whole-ness not learned or acquired through religion. In some ways, this is the outcome of many long conversations with Waagan (crow) who wanders around our neighbourhood, distributing his particular form of wisdom.

I am an Anglican priest for how much longer no one knows. I am Wiradjuri embedded by birth, Australian for purposes of management and control, and Anglican (Christian) because I had

---

18 Wiradjuri dictionary

no other choice. Our family history is such that we have no direct connections to a mob, except we know our great grandparents were Wiradjuri (great grandmother) and Kamilaroi/Kalkadoon (great grandfather).

They met in a blacks' camp that had been moved several times before my grandmother's birth and her being left behind at a young age with a local white family. Blacks' camps were like refugee camps for Aboriginal people. Removing people from country meant they had no place that was theirs, so they gathered together randomly on the edge of rural towns and villages.

She had described the situation with the family she was left with as one of being their slave for her first 18 years – doing a range of housekeeping and farm duties without a choice. There is no record that they adopted her, although she had their family name.

She described my grandfather as her knight on a white horse who rescued her. Having 10 children in a remote bush home 25 miles from town in the 1920s and '30s seems a little like slavery to me. She remained there long after my grandfather died, caring for odds and sods of Uncles until the mid-sixties, so the 'slavery' continued.

Not an unusual story but a story disconnecting us from lore, language, ritual and land. My grandfather insisted no one know about my grandmother's background, and we grew up as white people, although some of us were more suntanned than others. One of the ways to fit in was to practise Christianity. For my family, this was initially Presbyterian because my grandfather was Irish Protestant. For my immediate family, it was to become

Anglican with my father and brother. We were confirmed together at the time I would have been initiated into tribal lore.

Becoming Anglican was one of the whitest things a blackfella could do. Being an Anglican priest was and is the ultimate sign of assimilation, not just into the colonial culture as the Queen of England is the head of the church, but into the duality at the heart of Christianity.

Being Christian has never felt comfortable for me. During my early adulthood, I joined the Salvation Army and embraced its central belief that the sacrifice of an innocent man was to make me and all sinners (we were all sinners apparently) clean. The blood of Jesus washes white as snow we sang fervently, or, in my case, mumbled unconvincingly. Being white is the normative state for Christians, I guess.

The whole idea that someone had to die for my wrongdoings never sat well with me, and I wondered why. I wondered why God – the one who supposedly created this world – made people so 'bad' (read sinful) they needed someone sacrificed on their behalf. Why was he (always male) unable to resolve the relationship problem he had with humans caused by Adam and Eve, two imaginary people living in an imaginary Garden and accused of committing the original sin, without killing his only son?

These and other similar questions have never gone away. They remain; and I am unable to find convincing reasons I should ignore them. They have become central to my journey back to my inner indigenous self. Those intuitions I felt as a child, walking barefoot through the bush, sitting high in trees watching nature close up and feeling the dirt between my toes, remain. Feeling fully at home in that space and time all points to another way of living. Here is a philosophy without the need to kill others to be fully human and fully alive, a way to live an abundant life.

Over the last twenty years since I suddenly realised who I was after looking at a photograph of my wonderful grandmother and thinking, 'You idiot, and you thought Dad was that colour because he was sunburnt', I have engaged in re-engaging with what lives within me. Being Aboriginal has its own way of becoming you. It happens in bits and pieces, little bits here, fragments of connection and light there, and gradually you begin to evolve into whom you indeed are – an Aboriginal.

In this journey, I have found myself moving away from, or at least reading through different eyes, the Christian myth. It has expanded to include all my 'cousins' and the universe. It is about how we live with an urge for wholeness and balance expressed through proper and appropriate kinship relationships with all who share this planet. It is about finding patterns in the stories about Jesus in particular and connecting those patterns to gain the story under the story ad infinitum.

It has resulted in understanding that Aboriginal people are spiritual by virtue of their birth under a tree on country. Aboriginality encompasses lore, language, law, ceremony, and more, all of which are present in the country under our feet and all around us. It describes the way to be in every sphere of life. We do not become spiritual; we are spiritual, and our traditional manner of living allowed for this to become evident to the individual at the right times in their lives – through initiation, ceremony, ritual, and language.

Aboriginal people have no need for Christianity or spirituality as separate categories. They are their category. Damage, irreparable damage in many ways, has been done to this category by colonisation and genocide. We and all that defines us suffered replacement by the colonisers of the past – genocide, missions, the stolen generation, assimilation – and the neo-colonisers of the present – Northern Territory Emergency Intervention, the cash management card, the stolen generations version two, Closing the Gap and more.

It will take some time for us to regain our place as people. Much of the wisdom and innate capacity have been destroyed. We now have to work hard to restore what we once were – sovereign, autonomous custodians of the land and the universe, the space beyond us in every direction.

Returning to where I began. I woke up in dread because I have been talking about Aboriginal spirituality, and I have been untruthful. It does not exist as the western mind hears it. *Merriam Webster Dictionary* has the following inclusions in its definition of the word spirit:

Spirit:
- *an animating or vital principle held to give life to physical organisms the immaterial intelligent or sentient part of a person*
- *the activating or essential principle influencing a person*

Spiritual:
- *of, relating to, consisting of, or affecting the spirit*
- *related or joined in spirit*
- *of or relating to supernatural beings or phenomena*

Spirituality:
- *the quality or state of being spiritual.*[19]

I have selected these and not the numerous connections to religion, clergy, and evil spirits and more because these speak more truly of the essence I call Aboriginality. If we indeed use the term Aboriginal spirituality, it is in this framework, but not as a separate category of being; it is merely Aboriginal.

I may seem to be splitting hairs, but it is crucial we define ourselves and our understanding of ourselves and not others.

Mick Dodson writes:

> *Recognition of a peoples fundamental right to self determination must include the right to self-definition, and to be free from the control and manipulation of an alien people. It must include the right to inherit the collective identity of one's people, and to transform that identity creatively according to the self-determined aspirations of one's people and one's own generation. It must include the freedom to live outside the cage created by other people's images and projections.*[20]

Like my friend Waagan says, I am spiritual because I am Aboriginal, and the two are synonymous, not separate categories. They are one, and it is learning to live into that ones-ness that has become my Aboriginal journey.

---

19 Merriam-webster.com. (2019). *Definition of SPIRIT*. [online] Available at: https://www.merriam-webster.com/dictionary/spirit [Accessed 11 Sep. 2019].
20 Bamblett, L., Myers, F. and Rowse, T. (2019). *The difference identity makes*. 1st ed. Canberra: Aboriginal Studies Press, p. 47.

This book will address these and other matters relevant for anyone to begin, and – I say again – to start to get an insight into what being Aboriginal is. It is not grounded in traditional business, as I have never experienced initiation into my traditions; with my family connections and uncertainty, I need to be careful in doing so. It is grounded in the journey and the slow release of knowledge and wisdom as I find patterns and kinship connections as I grow older and wiser (just a little in both cases!)

This is not a definitive statement but a place to begin, to walk off from, sit down with, and to dialogue, listen to, engage with others on the same journey. I am not afraid to be wrong – I often am – but unless we have a go, we will never, never know.

As Tyson says, this is a journey 'us-two', you and I, people of faith and Aboriginal people, reader and author, indigenous and non-indigenous people need to take together.

Here is my hand. I invite you to walk with me. We will learn together.

A LITTLE BIT OF HISTORY

As an artist who happens to be indigenous, people perceive me as responsible for revealing the deep wisdom of our people through brushstrokes and colour on a piece of canvas. I and my art are treated differently from that of a non-indigenous artist. Society recognises this art for its artistic qualities alone and not its place in a separate art category. Unless my art speaks of or is suspected of speaking of some hidden indigenous insight into life, and fits a preconceived idea of Aboriginal art, then it is not judged on its merits but instead on its lacking.

Disappointing as it may be for you, the reader, I have no special Aboriginal or artistic hiddenness to share with you. I am like all indigenous people. I am like you. I am on a journey, and I am discovering Aboriginality[21] and artistic capability and coping with daily life one day at a time. Now I am an older person, there are some things I know, and I hope to share some of these with you.

Another interesting point – obvious but often not seen – the spirit world and art are not benign; it is not always beautiful colours telling uplifting stories or spiritual truths. The spirits will do what is required to wake us up, protect and direct us, and this will not always be comfortable or reassuring. Art that does not disturb you at some level is not doing its job. We, indigenous people, live in a world of levels or strata and patterns. The surface

---

21 As you will note as we move forward, I equate spirituality with Aboriginality. The reasons will become clear as you read.

image is one telling of the story contained in the layers beneath and creating the patterns appearing on the surface. Nothing is what it seems to be.

This complexity applies to identity, Aboriginality and art known broadly as Aboriginal or indigenous. This chapter will look at the impact of neo-colonial nostalgia in forming indigenous identity as it pertains to both spirituality and creativity. The premise is that ideas about Aboriginal art and spirituality – as perceived by non-indigenous people – continue the mediation of indigenous identity constructed under colonialism, and identifies people, spirituality and art from a continuing western perspective.

In terms of Aboriginal identity, Aboriginality sometimes called spirituality, the impact of Christianity in both replacing what makes Aboriginal people Aboriginal and influencing what we understand as indigenous spirituality, such as dadirri[22] or deep listening, is, arguably, undeniable. The indigenous life is the container and the contained in life and art, concluding that neither exists without the whole within the indigenous communal setting.

The indigenous experience is defined by the idea of Aboriginality, being Aboriginal in a universe containing you within it. As you are indigenous to the universe, you, in turn, hold it and all that exists within your body. You are who you were before you were born.

---

22 Facebook.com. (2019). *Dadirri - A Reflection by Miriam - Rose Ungunmerr- Baumann | Facebook.* [online] Available at: https://www.facebook.com/notes/australian-Aboriginal-directory/dadirri-a-reflection-by-miriam-rose-ungunmerr-baumann/10153007928998513/ [Accessed 13 Sep. 2019].

A Little Bit of History

It is crucial to remember that eighty-seven per cent of indigenous people living in this country B.C.P.[23] had been wiped out by genocide in a little over one hundred years.[24] Less than one hundred thousand people remained as a result of massacres, combat and disease. In some places, such as the Mudgee shire,[25] all tribal Aboriginals had been 'exterminated'[26] by 1876, just fifty years after the first massacre occured. In this case, those who were the perpetrators of the violence were pillars of society, donated land and funds to build and maintain the local Anglican church, this despite the fact that the first Rector had previously been in charge of the mission at Wellington, a neighbouring town. The only Aboriginal people in the area after that time were part of a Black's Camp at Wilpinjong, near Wollar, and had all come from somewhere else.

The majority of indigenous people who remained in this country were in central and northern Australia where the white supremacists either had no interest in land or were outnumbered, an issue the Northern Territory struggled with until the late twentieth century.

Colin Tatz develops the concept of genocide to describe the situation experienced by Aboriginal people in his excellent book, *Genocide in Australia*.[27] Genocide is a term that describes something more than a war or a massacre. It is the intentional act of eradicating both a people and their culture from the space

---

23 B.C.P. means Before Cook and Philip; A.C.P. is After Cook and Philip.
24 Kemp, C. and Loughrey, G. (2018). *A Voice in the Wilderness*. Sydney: Anglican Board of Mission - Australia Limited.
25 En.wikipedia.org. (2019). *Mudgee*. [online] Available at: https://en.wikipedia.org/wiki/Mudgee [Accessed 13 Sep. 2019].
26 Accredited to William Cox at Rylstone, N.S.W. in 1825.
27 Tatz, C. (n.d.). *Genocide in Australia*. Australian Institute of Aboriginal and Torres Strait Islander Studies (AIATSIS) 1999.

to which they are indigenous. The purposeful eradication of vermin, the clearing of the land of a species less than those who came here with a perceived superior culture and religion, is well documented elsewhere.

I contend that there could not have been a declared war because there was no one, under the doctrine of *Terra Nullius*, to declare war against; if the land was empty, there was no one here to fight. Besides, given the practice of land clearing, the title of war gives it a dignity and stature it does not deserve. War conjures up for the modern mind images of opposing armies and rules of war governing what is appropriate.

This understanding was not the mode of engagement here. Settlers and governments employed a range of brutal practices, including the poisoning of water supplies and flour rations, stirruping,[28] massacres, random shootings, and the use of Native Police. Tatz and others thoroughly document these.

While there is some case to argue that much of the destruction was done by out of control settlers carving out an existence in a new world and not by soldiers or governments, the fact remains that there was a pervading attitude across society implicitly permitting the genocide to occur.

Taken for their 'protection', particularly in the east and the south of the country, they found themselves in missions run by churches intent on replacing the pagan beliefs with their specific brand of Christianity. While the experience was different in the north, with many local missions and their overlords providing sanctuary for the local people, the trade-off was still the

---

28 A method of killing natives by swinging your stirrup at their head.

imposition of a new religion, often in its more fundamental or evangelical forms.

The fact was that these practices were protecting only the settlers. They were now able to get on with the stealing of country without the interference of the pesky natives. Along with this process of civilising, the savages were given education and the replacement of traditional language with English. It is not too harsh to say that we became the replacement people – what we had, knew and trusted were replaced – often brutally – by what was a purportedly superior way of being.

The process of assimilation continued through the period we now know as the Stolen Generations.[29] This period continued the complete annihilation of a culture, by removing children from families, forbidding indigenous cultural practice, spirituality and language. Assimilating the stolen children into the wider community facilitated the inculcation of a western and Christian world-view to both humanise and oversee the death of an entire race.

As a lighter-skinned Aboriginal, the prospect offered by assimilation was tempting. Many of us had no direct ancestral or tribal traditions, language or Aboriginality. We were adrift in a sea of whiteness, and it appeared to be a better option to become lost in that possibility than to continue in a world of racism and violence. It did not take long for me, and many of those like me, to work it out that we might be able to make an effort to assimilate but to those we began to move amongst we remained the outsider, 'once a blackfella always a blackfella'. The stereotype didn't and

---

29 En.wikipedia.org. (2019). *Stolen Generations*. [online] Available at: https://en.wikipedia.org/wiki/Stolen_Generations [Accessed 13 Sep. 2019].

hasn't changed, and one is faced with the sense that no matter how well you did, how hard you tried, you would never be good enough.

Almost all of our culture in the southern and eastern regions was lost. There were few elders left to pass on knowledge and practice, and we are playing catch up trying to find ourselves in this neo-colonial space. It is why people like me are not seen as real indigenous people because we lack colour, dirt, poverty and dot paintings.

Dr Marcus Bunyan suggests that 'Australia is not a post-colonial but a neo-colonial country. Imperialism as a concept and colonialism as a practice are still active in a new form'.[30] Post-colonialism refers to the ideologies and practices of an independent nation kicking off the strictures and structures of imperialism and developing a new way to wholeness where the previously marginalised become involved in the national discourse. Australia does not see this here.

Denying Aboriginal people a voice and the capacity to self-determine, based on an unceded sovereignty continues. Despite the debate on religious freedom and freedom of speech commenced in 2019, such freedoms have been, and continue to be, denied Aboriginal people. The government and western white culture still choose to act and interfere in the life, art and culture of Aboriginal people, denying them their voice on equal terms. Events such as the 2007 Northern Territory Intervention, the introduction of the cash management card and the refusal of the

---

30 Bunyan, M. (2019). [online] Artblart.files.wordpress.com. Available at: https://artblart.files.wordpress.com/2013/07/un-settling-Aboriginality-dr-marcus-bunyan-july-2013.pdf [Accessed 13 Sep. 2019], p.4;

A Little Bit of History

voice heard in the *Statement of The Heart*, points to a continuing colonial approach to identity and culture. The government remains in control of 'subjugated people', and white ideas, values and religion retain their supremacy in defining what and who is Aboriginal or not. Australia remains a colony of the motherland. This newer form of colonialism remains profoundly racist, tied to the remnants of the White Australia policy.

To be genuinely post-colonial, both sides of this process need liberation at the same time. Bunyan writes, 'Aboriginal communities are still thought incapable of taking an active role in shaping and administering their own communities' and retaining sovereignty over their art, culture and spirituality.[31] As in colonial times, the definition of these factors remains with, or at the very least, mediated through non-indigenous colonial thought and concepts.

Not only is this a tragedy for us as Aboriginal people, but it is also a tragedy for those who came here after Cook and Philip. The sins of the fathers (and mothers) are continuing to flow down through the generations, and without a new beginning, genocidal colonialism will continue. Forgiving our communal sins can only occur via a transformative moment shared by all.

---

31 Bunyan, M. (2019). [online] Artblart.files.wordpress.com. Available at: https://artblart.files.wordpress.com/2013/07/un-settling-Aboriginality-dr-marcus-bunyan-july-2013.pdf [Accessed 13 Sep. 2019], p. 5.

IN THE GOOD OLD DAYS

Neo-colonial nostalgia is critical to what we now understand as indigenous identity, spirituality and art. Nostalgia is more than looking back with rose-coloured glasses. Based on the work of Svetlana Boym,[32] Jean Starobinsky[33] and Johannes Hofer,[34] nostalgia is seen to have two major categories – reconstructive or reflective.

Reconstructive nostalgia is that which looks back to a time deemed to be worthy of reconstruction in the present. It often refers to a time one has not experienced but is evident in the lives of those who went before us. It is the form of nostalgia we see in the election of populist conservatives, in Brexit and the push for religious freedom and free speech in our own country. The last two because the glory days of Christianity have passed and is under threat, engendering a drive to return to the good old days when you could participate in genocide and force all to accept your belief system. Interestingly, indigenous people were denied freedom of religion throughout our nation's history and are still without freedom of speech to this day.

It is not merely a colonial nostalgia; it is present within the indigenous community as well. Many disenfranchised people

---

32 Boym, S. (2016). *The future of nostalgia*. New York: Basic Books, a member of the Perseus Books Group.
33 En.wikipedia.org. (2019). *Jean Starobinski*. [online] Available at: https://en.wikipedia.org/wiki/Jean_Starobinski [Accessed 13 Sep. 2019].
34 En.wikipedia.org. (2019). *Hans Johannes Hofer*. [online] Available at: https://en.wikipedia.org/wiki/Hans_Johannes_Hofer [Accessed 13 Sep. 2019].

who have not experienced traditional life but have heard about it, pine for a return to the days when it was the normal and life seemed more straightforward. Arguably, this is the underpinning of the campaign for a treaty, voice and the *Statement of the Heart*. People are seeking a return to those days when indigenous people were free to be and do as tradition directs. As this is a time that no longer exists, they are seeking a return to traditions many do not know nor have experienced. Colonialism has mediated much of what they now understand as tradition.

Reflective nostalgia looks back at the same period and compares it with now and works to divine truths from both places. It is a collaborative and continuing work that – unlike reconstructive nostalgia – accepts that there may be no definitive answer or solution. It relies heavily on methodologies such as story work to bring people together. It is comfortable with uncertainty and working with what is now to find a path into the future.

Reconstructive nostalgia is at work in neo-colonialism. It desires a return to the time when power was power, and those without it remained outsiders. While raw power is no longer acceptable, the interference of governments and the rule of the academy are instrumental in maintaining the impact of control and imperialism. A recent exception in Australia is the 2007 Northern Territory Intervention. Here raw power was used, both within parliament to suspend the human rights statute, and to use the military in seizing peoples' property and rights.

Reconstructive nostalgia is at work in art and Aboriginality. It seeks to maintain that indigenous people are the exotic outsider who have a 'special place' in our corporate memory but not deemed equal to the dominant forms and culture. It is revered for its difference but is not special enough to hold its own with western art or to stand without the crutch of Christianity.

Indigenous spirituality had to be replaced and continues to be replaced by Christianity, a fact that has doomed our form of being to a lingering extinction in its original way. We speak instead of indigenous theology and indigenous Christianity, both – I would contend – collaborate with the project of neo-colonialism and cultural genocide and are not Aboriginal.

In simplistic terms, neo-colonial nostalgia is the reality for Aboriginal art, culture and Aboriginality. For our purposes, we will concentrate on art and spirituality. Richard Bell has coined the term "OoogaBooga Art" to describe remote indigenous art. He argues 'that it is based upon a false notion of tradition that casts Indigenous people as the exotic other, produced under the white, primitivist gaze'.[35] I would agree with his assumption based on the comments I hear about «real Aboriginal art» and the answer to questions to students about what is Aboriginal art – the response, it has a lot of dots.

There is no traditional Aboriginal art form as the Western mind understands it. There are traditional stories, which have been told down through the ages via the oral tradition but rarely drawn for posterity. Art and symbol were used for ritual, ceremony and education, for a distinct purpose, but never for the other, only for the community. It appeared on certain specific items, body paint and drawn in the dirt but was never made solely as an item to trade or sell. It had no value other than the value attributed

---

35   Bunyan, M. (2019). [online] Artblart.files.wordpress.com. Available at: https://artblart.files.wordpress.com/2013/07/un-settling-Aboriginality-dr-marcus-bunyan-july-2013.pdf [Accessed 13 Sep. 2019].

to it by the community. Aboriginal art is communal; it is for the building up of sovereignty.

What is seen as traditional art today comes as a construct from the early 1970s and the commencement of acrylic painting of stories by the Central Desert art 'school'. In the Eastern states, there is evidence of indigenous art practice to gain income and control over the Aboriginal identity early in the twentieth century. Despite this, the 1970s remain the significant tipping point for the Aboriginal art industry.[36] From those humble beginnings, it has grown into an industry, making many non-indigenous people financially independent and, fortunately, sustaining many Aboriginal communities.

It has provided an avenue for indigenous people to find a place in neo-colonialism without giving up their identity. They have sought to give the white man what he wanted while not surrendering the secrets of their dreaming and sovereignty in the process.

Art is a way for the white western community to bestow identity on Aboriginal people, to mark who is a real Aboriginal artist or whose art is authentic or not. I know this personally for it's the question I answer when I enter a gallery – 'Are you traditional or urban?' 'Urban.' 'Sorry, only trade in traditional art.'

Are those of us who do not paint what are seen as traditional stories and use art to challenge the white hegemony any less an Aboriginal artist than Bell's 'OoogaBooga Artists'? Are we not

---

36   Kleinert, S. (2019). *"Jacky Jacky Was a Smart Young Fella": A study of art and Aboriginality in south-east Australia 1900-1980*. [online] Openresearch-repository.anu.edu.au. Available at: https://openresearch-repository.anu.edu.au/handle/1885/9329 [Accessed 13 Sep. 2019].

doing out loud what they are doing less obviously by using the system to earn income while hiding the true meaning of paintings, perhaps creating stories for the art world? Both are responses to the continuing colonialism we endure. I would suggest we are both modern contemporary Australian artists who wish, at some point, to lose the tag of Aboriginal and be recognised on the same level as similar artists in the endless stream of art.

In reading art produced by indigenous people and, in particular, communally created art, it is essential to remember that what appears on the surface is just the template for deep storytelling. As Chris Sarra[37] has suggested in a paper presented to the 2018 Brotherhood of St Laurence Dinner, we have a stratified identity and our stories have stratified meanings. Traditional stories have numerous interpretations and can be used to teach, explain and untangle several different aspects of life, often very different from the title given and the beauty that first meets the eye.

To be able to understand this process, one needs to approach art and those who created the art with the seven principles of 'story work' seeing (research) suggested by Jo-Ann Archibald.[38] The seven principles are respect, responsibility, reverence, reciprocity, holism, interrelatedness and synergy. This type of art takes time (for me, often a minimum of 3 months), lived experience and learning to produce, and contains many different stories demanding adherence to these principles as a viewer. If you spend only the average time people spend in front of art in

---

37 Sarra, C. (2019). *Sambell Oration Dinner 2018*. [online] Available at: https://www.bsl.org.au/events/sambell-oration-dinner-2018/ [Accessed 13 Sep. 2019].
38 Decolonising Research: Indigenous Story Work as Methodology, Loddon: Zed Books 2019. p. 1.

galleries – roughly three or so minutes – then there is no way for you to gain the wisdom the ancients have placed in the piece.

In terms of Aboriginality or spirituality, much the same applies.

Several years ago, I was present at a conference at Alice Springs for non-indigenous people on the 'spiritual journey'. Miriam Rose Ungemurr was the principal speaker. What I witnessed was a group of people seeking to gain exclusive insight into the spiritual realm by listening to her speak about Dadirri, deep listening. They were transfixed, waiting for the droplets of wisdom to fall upon them and transform them there and then. Late the next year, I shared in a conversation with Miriam and witnessed the same thing.

I receive regular requests to teach or talk about deep listening, and my reply is, 'You do not have enough time. It has taken us 65,000 years of life experience and under the guidance of our elders to get this far. And you want me to teach it in a 2-hour session?' Deep listening is not Christian meditation, although it appears to be same. It is not mindfulness, though it seems to be the same. It is not spiritual as understood by Christians and others. It is not otherworldly. It is this worldly, the world beneath our feet and in which we live, the world coming down the road towards us. It is a way of life that sustains. It is what it means to be Aboriginal.

There is no disconnection in Aboriginal thought between the ordinary and the spiritual. The spiritual is evident in the repository of wisdom, our sacred texts, the dirt that lies deep under our feet and defines our country. My father would say, 'Listen to your country, and it will tell you what you need and what it needs'. You cannot become spiritual if you are Aboriginal. You are spiritual because you are Aboriginal.

Why?

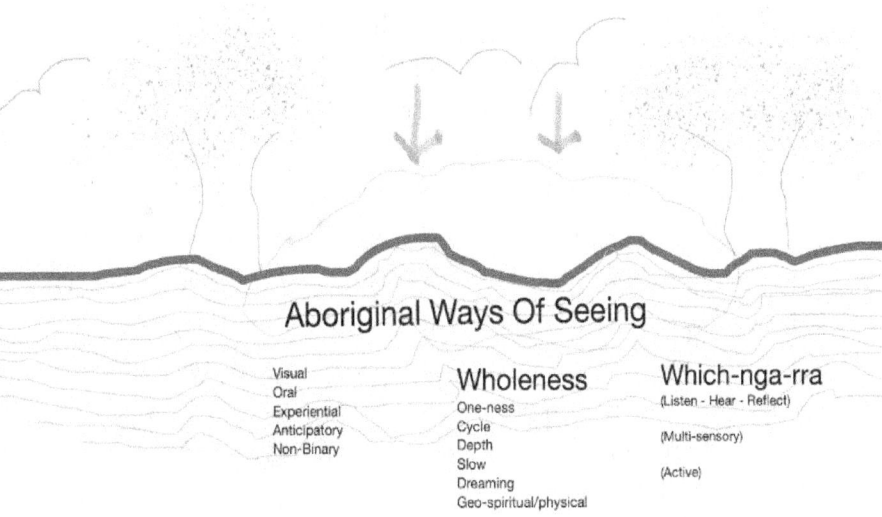

(Even the spellchecker is neo-colonial – 'which' should be 'whin'. I didn't change it as it makes a point.)

Aboriginality is a way of seeing and it is demonstrated in this drawing. Interestingly, western spell checkers are confused by Wiradjuri language and change the words to suit.

We are born under a tree on country and carry that country in our body until we die. Dying, we return to the land beneath our feet, adding our story and its various patterns and layers to layers already there. We become part of the repository of wisdom and trauma, which reappears in the lives that follow us.

Our country contains us, and we hold our country, its pain and wisdom, in our lives. We live each day attempting to reconcile the past and our present to lessen the impact on the future. Jeanette Armstrong, in her paradigm of identity, suggests this is 'how localised people interact with the land to gain wisdom and knowledge so that life may continue to perpetuate in a continuous cycle of regeneration on the land for all life forms, not just humans'.[39]

Spirituality and art come together through story. Indigenous people are story people. We make meaning for ourselves through the stories we tell ourselves. The stories are multi-layered and stratified. They carry different meanings according to the purposes they fulfil. Our contemporary art has been used as a vehicle to tell story and illuminate our Aboriginality – what it means to be indigenous in this place and time.

These stories are told primarily for the community, for those whose sovereignty it exemplifies. They are not stories for outsiders, rarely understood in terms of the depth and complexity they hold. They are, for them, just pretty Aboriginal pictures.

Those who hold the country in their bodies and transfer that into story on canvas, paper, pottery, basket weaving or human form do so as spiritual beings. In themselves, the art pieces are not spiritual; they simply hold the story for those who are of country, who are spiritual, to read and enact.

---

39 Christian, Dorothy, 'Decolonising Research' in Archibald Jo-Ann (ed.), *Indigenous Storywork*. Vancouver: UBC Press.

Those of us who paint modern storylines – what may be called in some cases trauma lines – paint with a similar sense of pattern and layers but tell a different story to that seen as traditional. Our art may symbolise reflective nostalgia, and the spirituality found therein comes from within the indigenous person who is painting the story. Those who paint explicit Christian stories using Aboriginal symbols and types or paint traditional images with Christian symbols and types, run the risk of painting neo-colonial stories while trying to make sense of the intersection between the two spiritualities.

The two worldviews are very different. One is theo-physical – up and out with an interventionist creator. The other is geo-physical, as noted in the diagram used earlier. While we can use ideas and images from both, once we do so, those ideas and images lose their authentic nature. Art in indigenous thinking is closely related to and dependent upon language and oral tradition and less on the western concept of aesthetics. It is to be read, not looked at for its beauty or skill.

Both Aboriginality and art are ordinary, practical, mysterious and purposeful, holding within the 'great other'. Both are communal and not individual, existing to maintain the sovereignty of people into the future.

ON BEING ABORIGINAL

To answer the question I asked in the beginning: perhaps, there is simply no such category as Aboriginal spirituality? I contacted Robert Dixon,[40] a linguist at Charles Sturt University and asked is there a word in any Aboriginal language or dialect for spirituality? His reply: 'Sorry, I don't know of such a word. This is a very European concept'.

What does this do to the idea of Aboriginal spirituality? Is it a useful category or merely a settler label used to name the unique way of seeing, witnessed in the colonised people? Is this usage only a way to address what is mysterious and disturbing to the Western mind? Is it so beyond comprehension that a civilisation deemed to be inferior has such a complex social structure and underpinning traditions that, instead of embracing the mystery, we consign it to the grab bag of labels and label its essential essence spirituality? We don't understand how this intricate and multi-layered culture works and, anyway, it is an inferior culture of deficit, this complexity cannot be real, it must have to do with the myth of the spiritual kind.

I would suggest that a category such as Aboriginal spirituality may not be helpful. It masks the real value and potential Aboriginal culture offers for the enrichment of the broader Australian society. Spirituality, as we have noted earlier, is deemed to be a personal choice, although one could argue we are all open to being so

---

40 Dixon, R. (2019). *Australia's Original Languages - An Introduction*. 1st ed. Sydney: Allen & Unwin.

by nature. To use this category in a pan-Aboriginal sense to encompass those parts of Aboriginal culture we don't understand separates people from what makes them who they are. It is our way of seeing that makes us able to be sovereign custodians of our sovereign lands and not merely exhibits in a cultural freak show.

Aboriginality is a disputed space. Who defines who is Aboriginal, and what are the categories they use to do so? Janice McRanald has asked the question, 'Who has the permission to think and speak and who gives them that permission?'[41] This concept applies here. Who has permission to be Aboriginal and who gives them that permission? Do those who give that permission then retain the right to vet and categorise Aboriginality according to imposed, different colonising categories?

While writing this book, some raised this issue concerning Professor Bruce Pascoe.[42] It was alleged by such as Andrew Bolt[43] and Josephine Cashman that there was no evidence Pascoe was, as he says, a Yuin[44] man. Cashman referred her concerns to the Minister for Home Affairs in the Australian Government since 2017, Peter Dutton[45] who then referred it to the Australian Federal Police. The accusation was that Pascoe was not Aboriginal and therefore had benefited via employment and reputation by fraudulently posing as an Aboriginal. Cashman, as reported in

---

41 Paper presented at St Francis Theological College, Brisbane, commenting on my book *Another Time, Another Place – Towards an Australian Church*, July 2019.
42 En.wikipedia.org. (2020). *Bruce Pascoe*. [online] Available at: https://en.wikipedia.org/wiki/Bruce_Pascoe [Accessed 11 Jan. 2020].
43 En.wikipedia.org. (2020). *Andrew Bolt*. [online] Available at: https://en.wikipedia.org/wiki/Andrew_Bolt [Accessed 11 Jan. 2020].
44 En.wikipedia.org. (2020). *Yuin*. [online] Available at: https://en.wikipedia.org/wiki/Yuin [Accessed 11 Jan. 2020].
45 En.wikipedia.org. (2020). *Peter Dutton*. [online] Available at: https://en.wikipedia.org/wiki/Peter_Dutton [Accessed 11 Jan. 2020].

The Australian on Saturday 11 January 2020, suggested leaving the identification to clans and community groups and the development of a register of all who are genuine Aboriginals.

Here is a profoundly concerning neo-colonial development which will maintain the doctrine of deficit about our people and mean that the many who could identify, won't. It will also mean that the collective benefit of those who have found success and middle-class credibility in the broader community that is Australia cannot add to the cultural capital available for all to use. The idea of cosmopolitanism and an Aboriginal middle-class as suggested by Stan Grant[46] in his writings will only receive validation if those who make it here are on the list of real Aboriginals proposed by Cashman and co. As noted elsewhere, I am not one of those easily fitted into the Aboriginal world as suggested and will undoubtedly find myself having to defend my own identity. After a lifetime of coming to grips with this identity and taking the precarious step of «outing» myself, it now seems that I am not black enough to be Aboriginal but not white enough to be white!

While I understand that this is a complex issue driven by several different concerns, one is the way of distributing Aboriginal funding in this Australia by Governments. Primary funding for regions is attached to the number of people identifying as Aboriginal. If the number of people who do not fit the "stereotype" identify as Aboriginal (urban, light-skinned, educated, home-owning etc.), funding may be diverted away from those most in need (dark-skinned, living in remote communities, perceived to be real traditional people, poor, etc.) This is a separate issue to identity. It is about who has access to funds and who can control or give permission to be Aboriginal.

---

46   Grant, S. (2019). *Australia Day*. Surry Hills, NSW: HarperCollins Australia / RHYW.

Bronwyn Carlson has written an excellent book, *The Politics of Identity* which both researches and explains the complexity involved. It is not black or white, but that is what it has been reduced to. In her final chapter, she has this to say about this period of surveillance of who is in and who is out by both Aboriginal communities and the more comprehensive Government and political communities:

> There is in this web evidence that there is no pinpoint where blame or responsibility can be placed on the current struggle in which we are all involved, beyond the injustice of colonisation. We all uphold Aboriginal community practices when we fail to question the constitutive parameters of community relations with the nation-state and the role of community authority of Aboriginal bodies. We all uphold community practice in the way we support the singular choices to be or not to be Aboriginal. We all uphold community practice in the way we support the imposition of what are essentially membership rules on something so important and fundamental to the human psyche and sense of wellbeing as a person's individual identity. And while we uphold these things in the name of collective solidarity, we overlook the curtailment of individual freedom to be all of who we now are after over two hundred years of disruption and varied experiences. **In the process, we continue to deny some Aboriginal people their particular history of being Aboriginal and what it now means to them.**[47] *(Bold type is mine.)*

---

[47] Carlson, B. *The Politics of Identity*, Canberra: Aboriginal Studies Press, 2016.

Western thinking categorises and labels what we don't understand or what is wild and untamed, outside our regular view or perception of the world. Modern human beings, as rational enlightenment figures, need to tame the world or the exotic or at least bring them under our sphere of influence so that they do not unduly disturb our existence. This was and remains the colonising project, and Aboriginal people are not alone in this process – those of different ethnicities, genders, gender identification, disabilities and more find themselves colonised to ensure the dominant culture remains in power.

Robert Dixon confirmed what woke me up in the night – the realisation that I have been using a Western Christian category to explain or place what it means to be Aboriginal in a safe type. It is a means of taming what we cannot understand, what does not fit comfortably in neo-colonial nostalgia. We have a Dewey number style system for all things and being Aboriginal goes into 'spirituality' and is cross-referenced to the 'exotic' and 'traditional', amongst others that are not nearly as complimentary as these.

When one is designated Aboriginal, it is usually to identify the difference and not similarity, diversity in a negative sense. Speaking to a group of people about these matters, a gentleman asked, "Are all Aboriginal people able to articulate these things in the same way you do?" The implicit assertion was: are all Aboriginal people as articulate as you or are you an exception? In other words, are all Aboriginal people stupid except you?

At the same gathering, a woman who claimed to be concerned about Aboriginal matters came up to me and said, in the ensuing conversation, 'What can we do? We cannot give Aboriginal people money. They will only spend it on drugs and alcohol?' I had just spoken for twenty minutes, and she failed to see she was talking about me. The fact that several bottle-shops are doing a roaring trade in her local area and possibly only one or two families of our people are nearby seemed to elude her.

As an artist, I am aware that there is a style of art deemed to be appropriate Aboriginal art. Aboriginal artists create both but what passes as Aboriginal art is judged, not by us, but by the dominant society. If it has a lot of dots and refers to 'my country' or some form of dreaming, then it may well pass. Art with a distinctively modern, no dots, and often pointing out the trauma lines that run through our country fails the test of being indigenous in the gabaa's eyes.

Light coloured indigenous people also do not fit the category of 'real' Aborigines. Often it is met with you are half/quarter/whatever caste, mixed blood or simply not accepted at all. People have rolled their sleeves up and placed their arm against mine to prove their point – you are not Aboriginal. The increased amount of melanin in one's skin only indicates you were born from people closer to the equator, not whether you are Aboriginal. Yet skin colour is deemed sufficient to categorise and label.

There are other examples of this type of naming and shaming. We like our Aboriginal people to do the exotic dancing or didgeridoo playing at our special events, kick footy goals for our team or be number one in tennis. It is also great when – wonder and amazement! – Aboriginal people get degrees, PhDs, become doctors and lawyers and enter parliament. Still, we do not want them to have the right to own their sovereignty and their autonomy as a people and to make decisions about what it means to be Aboriginal.

White Australia continues to do that. (If we let them.)

You are spiritual because of your identity as an Aboriginal. You're Aboriginal because you have no choice but to be. It is born in you. You're spiritual because that is part of your DNA. It comes with you into this world and remains with you until you leave, regardless of what you do with it.

Being Aboriginal is how you see yourself, the world, others and the Universe and it guides, teaches and ensures that you act out of respect and hospitality to all. You view the world through the lens of your indigeneity as a means of making sense of what is foreign and otherworldly to the world you know.

In the preface to her book, *Becoming Indigenous to the Universe*, Kerry Arebena writes as follows:

> ...it was critically important for me not to write as an "Indigenous scholar" but write about being indigenous to the Universe through scholarly activity, without being marginalised or made different because of indigeneity. (...) I have attempted to develop a continuum of indigenousness. The place I started from – my experience of being an Indigenous person in Australia – separates you (the reader) and me as being different; being indigenous to the Universe means that I am not separate from you. In fact, I have come to understand that as we are all indigenous of the Universe, we are deeply and profoundly connected.[48]

---

48 Arabena, K. (2015). *Indigenous to the Universe*. Melbourne: Australian Scholarly Publishing, pp. xiii-xiv.

We will return to the idea of being indigenous to the Universe later in this book, suffice to say, at this point, that any indication academics and creatives are Aboriginal places them in a different category to non-indigenous academics and creatives. My experience suggests we should avoid this naming of Aboriginality as a means of separation from the mainstream, even though it is vital to their practice. Without this way of seeing, there is no-thing new to see here.

When I started painting, I identified myself as Aboriginal. When I spoke at events, I used language as a means of letting people know who I am. It was a bit much for the man who attempted to leave the front row only to be dragged back by his wife and made to sit through the next twenty minutes of my talk!

Your being Aboriginal changes the way you see the world. You are deeply connected to the country as your databank or sacred text of knowledge, and you are informed by your relationships to others and live with a communal, not an individual focus, identifying with the kinship matrix, language groupings, ceremony and law.

They come not as individual elements overseen by different groups such as is the case in Western society; they are entwined and come as one unique package – you.

You stand at the centre and the margins of society and see it from a range of perspectives. Being a man, in my case, it is as sometimes a son, sometimes a father, sometimes a brother, sometimes an uncle, sometimes a husband and sometimes as a combination of one or more of those, concerning my kin. It is a journey from the particular to the Universe and back again.

In this journey, your responsibility is to act to enhance the community – the country from which you come. You are born under a tree to live in such a way that when you return under a tree, you place into the ground wisdom, knowledge and reconciliation in order that future generations will benefit.

You do this through such experiences as knowledge transfer and initiation, the gradual maturation into a senior man or woman of country. It is not about personal success but that of the community. Any progress is shared with all, including the conscious non-human kin who share space with you.

Aboriginal ways of seeing are not only about people. It is about the proper relationship with all creatures, ensuring all have what they need for survival and existence. All are citizens of the Universe, and just as you and I share connections because of that, we share links directly with them.

> *To be Aboriginal is many things and different to all. But at this moment, to me, it includes to follow a path to those who journeyed before you, similar but different, to hear the secret and loving stories of the land with understanding, to be independent, to hear and see with feeling that which cannot be seen with open eyes, be part of a group, be as natural as the land, and to be hospitable and enjoy hospitality.*[49]

You are spiritual because you are born of the earth and the Universe and are responsible for a particular and universal set of

---

49 Source: Aboriginal Identity: Who is 'Aboriginal'? - Creative Spirits, retrieved from https://www.creativespirits.info/Aboriginalculture/people/Aboriginal-identity-who-is-Aboriginal

relationships. It is a way of seeing all of life as a gift, and that gift can only be lived out through the essence of your Aboriginality.

This anonymous quote sums up what it means to be Aboriginal:

> *Being Aboriginal is not the colour of your skin or how broad your nose is. It is a spiritual feeling, an identity you know in your heart... It is a unique feeling that is difficult for non-Aboriginal to fully understand.*[50]

---

50 https://ideapod.com/10-Aboriginal-australian-quotes-will-change-perspective-life/

THIS GROUND, SHE'S MY MOTHER

Dyiramadilynabadhu Wiradjuri, yuwinnahdi Glenn.
I am proud to be Wiradjuri, and my name is Glenn.

Aboriginal people carry the imprint of country. "Where you from?" is the standard question we ask each other when we first meet. Not what is your name, but what is your country? "Where you from" is another way of saying what is your country and who is your mob? Names are variable. Country is not.

Knowing someone's country allows us to see where they fit with our mob and us, if there is a connection, where that connection is and how we are to interact with that person. It is our passport, and we carry it in our body and our being. We are always to remember "our land is as sacred as yourself, as a person like you are... The land and the people are the same. Same."[51]

Catherine Liddle writes:

> *Trying to frame this concept in modern language is like trying to grasp a two dimensional cup out of a piece of paper, it's the layers that make the cup palpable, not the drawing of it. Connection to country is inherent, we are born to it, it is how we identify ourselves, it is our family, our laws, our responsibility, our inheritance and our legacy.*[52]

---

51 Turner, M., McDonald, B. and Dobson, V. (2010). *Iwenhetyerrtye*. Alice Springs, N.T.: IAD Press.
52 https://www.sbs.com.au/nitv/article/2015/10/22/. (2019). *why-connection-*

Country is not a possession owned and operated by a group of people even though words like estate, tenure and laws can give that sense. It is a gift and a responsibility bequeathed by those who have benefited from its largesse. It is now in the continuing care of those people through those who come before them. It is an "everywhere, when" concept; it was, it is, and it will be.

Arabena suggests "country is used to describe the essence of the natural and other values that Aboriginal and Torres Strait Islander peoples have for their land, for where they come from and the distinctive roles and responsibilities that people have for their country".[53] Country is more than just a place or homeland. It defines a place and all found in and from there, no matter where that may be.

> Country means far more than just the physical landscape. Rather it '...incorporates people, animals, plants, water and land.

> But Country is more than just people and things; it is also what connects them to each other and the multiple spiritual and symbolic realms. It relates to laws, custom, movement, song, knowledge, histories, presents and futures. Country can be talked to, it can be known, it can itself communicate, feel and take action'.[54]

---

country-so-important-Aboriginal-communities. [online] Available at: https://www.sbs.com.au/nitv/article/2015/10/22/why-connection-country-so-important-Aboriginal-communities [Accessed 19 Sep. 2019].

53 Arabena, K. (2015). *Indigenous to the Universe.* Melbourne: Australian Scholarly Publishing, p.xxi
54 Cole-Hawthorne, R., Jones, D. and Low Choy, D. (2019). *An Aboriginal Obligation to Country: Challenging the Status Quo.* [online] Core.ac.uk. Available at: https://core.ac.uk/reader/143900511 [Accessed 12 Sep.

This Ground, She's My Mother

When writing about Spanish landscape painting, John Berger reflected that every landscape has an address and it is undeniably present in any representation of that place.[55] In a sense, this is the connection people have with country.[56] Every person has an address, and it is more than their place of abode, it is the very fibre of their being, a filament of thought or whisper of a word. It is them. They are the country writ large.

This is evident in the following quote from Riley Young, a Yarralin man, (who) spoke of the living earth as the giver of life:

> *Blackfellow never change him... We been borning (in) this country. We been grown up in this country. We been walkabout this country. We know this country all over.... Blackfella been born on top of that ground, and blackfella blood (in the ground)...This ground is mother. This ground, she's my mother. She's the mother for everybody. We born on top of this ground. This (is) our mother. That's why we worry about this ground.*[57]

The ground holds the sacred text; it contains within all the wisdom that has ever been and ever will be. We are born out of it and bring that wisdom with us, and when we die, we return to it to add our sentence to the pages held there. To damage the ground in any way is like ripping pages out of a religion's sacred text or pages out of a country's constitution. There is no replacing it. Once damaged, it is gone. It is why elders speaking against mining say, "Do not dig us up".

2019]. (Wright et al., 2012, p. 54)
55   Berger, J. and Overton, T. (2017). Portraits. London: Verso.
56   https://www.sbs.com.au/nitv/article/2015/10/22/. (2019). why-connection-country-so-important-Aboriginal-communities. [online]
57   Arabena, K. (2015). Indigenous to the Universe. Melbourne: Australian Scholarly Publishing, p. 21

> *(Country) is a cosmic model, it is a forest, an assembly of kin and allies, a womb, a grave, a tortoise, a microcosm in which every part is named and every relationship between parts is seen as a coherent whole.* [58]

Country is not just about dirt. We use it to include all that is above the ground for as far as the eye can see in any direction. It is cosmic and consists of the Universe – solar systems, planets, stars, comets and all created beings. Country is a relationship not restricted to people. The stars above your head guide travel from one place to another. It divines the seasons and explains when it is right to do a ceremony, plant crops, catch fish and eat kangaroo.

Country is not a romantic concept we hold as part of our identification of the exotic outsider. It is the concept of ancient people alive today in the lives of individuals and communities. It keeps the collective sense of belonging and shares it with all, and if cared for according to tradition, it will care for those it gave birth to – the people, creatures, land and all it holds. Traditionally 'no-thing' exists on country unless it was born there. 'Every-thing' born on country is country.

I am my country

Bronwyn Fredericks, in her must-read paper, *'We don't leave our identities at the city limits': Aboriginal and Torres Strait Islander people living in urban localities* states:

---

[58] Arabena, K. (2015). *Indigenous to the Universe*. Melbourne: Australian Scholarly Publishing, p.100

> *We don't leave our identities at a petrol station, bus stop, jetty or airport when we enter the city limits. When we live in a city or town, we don't become any less or any more Indigenous. Some of us even belong to the Country where huge cityscapes and towns have been built. Yet Aboriginal and Torres Strait Islander people living in urban areas are sometimes perceived as 'fake', 'not real' and 'not authentic' because 'real' Aboriginal people belong 'out back', 'on communities' and in the 'bush', and 'real' Torres Strait Islanders really live 'on islands' in the Torres Strait.*[59]

> *Bob Morgan states that 'my culture and worldview are centred in Gumilaroi land and its people. This is who I am and will always be. I am my country.'*[60]

Country is key to an indigenous person's identity. It is the country in which we develop relationships, find ourselves and discover our responsible place. The act of being responsible for culture, the land beneath your feet and those you share the earth with, is your work, your meaning, your hope.

This work is your responsibility to country. It takes work to live within the complexity of communal life and fulfil all required of you. It is valuable work as it adds to the cultural capital of the group and grows the capacity for survival and being. Without the work involved in maintaining kinship groups, providing for food and hospitality, fulfilling cultural and ceremonial requirements

---

59 Fredericks, B. (2019). 'We don't leave our identities at the city limits': Aboriginal and Torres Strait Islander people living in urban localities. [online] Core.ac.uk. Available at: https://core.ac.uk/reader/16294495 [Accessed 12 Sep. 2019].
60 Fredericks, B. (2019).

and for learning and transferring knowledge, the fabric of this robust society is at risk.

Fredericks concludes her paper by making the statement "we as Aboriginal people have the agency to define place and space as ours". She writes:

> We enact sovereignty through reconnection to places and landscape shaping, re-shaping and re-making, including the use of signs, symbols, images and representations to assert our connection and ownership.[61]

The modern economic system does not recognise this work. It is seen only as evidence of a deficit and inadequate culture outside the needs of consumerism. In a society not committed to possessions and wants, this work is valuable to all on country and needs to be understood as such. Not to do so leaves people lost, out of sync with the only way of being they know – know as being the knowledge passed down.

Even we as a people rarely understand this work. We applaud those who become successful in gabaa's world, becoming doctors, lawyers, teachers, sportspeople or artists, but we do not welcome the knowledge keepers, those who maintain our traditions. Regardless of my success in white peoples world, I am not in the same category as these people are.

We send little children away to the big cities to prop up the guilt-ridden institutions, religions and governments who need to help the poor black kids to show everyone they care. Do we know what we are doing? We are destroying our own culture as these

---

61 Fredericks, B. (2019).

young people miss vital stages in their tribal education, and if it doesn't turn out well in the big city, we get back kids who see themselves as failing. They should not have been there in the first place. Why do we not value ourselves?

Being on country embeds in us and animates what is naturally in us in such a way we become country. It begins when we are born and take our first breath of the place integral to our existence. There are stories of the old people leaving babies on the ground for a short while after the birth to bond (as we would say today) with their mother. At that moment, all that will be needed for life is, in a sense, 'uploaded' into the child's body and comes to life over their life.

This process of being born on country is often spoken of as being born under a tree on country and ensures you receive your Aboriginal being-ness. A friend works in a remote community and was advocating on behalf of a local lady with Centrelink. The conversation went something like this:

>   Centrelink: *Where was she born?*
>   Friend: *Where were you born?*
>   Lady: *Under the tree.*
>   Friend: *Under the tree.*
>   Centrelink: (Pause) *Can't put that down.* (Pause) *Does she have an address where she was born?*
>   Friend: *Do you have an address where you were born?*
>   Lady: *Under the tree. My brother from a different mother was born under the tree on the same day.*
>   Friend: *Nope. Under the tree.* (Pause) *Just put down 1 Main Street.*
>   Centrelink: *Can't. You just made that up.*

Friend: *Well, it's either that or under the tree!*

I am not sure how this conversation ended, but the lady was definite about her birthplace and her identity. They are one and not two distinct ideas. In this conversation, we also see a hint of the complicated relationships or kinship indicated by her "brother from a different mother".

Somewhere in my reading, I read a quote from an indigenous woman who said, "I carry my country in my body", insinuating that wherever you are you retain country. More importantly, you are never off country, which is right for me. While I am rarely on my country and have only briefly passed across my great-great-grandfathers land, what came with me, what I learnt from father and others is alive and speaking within me today. It may have lain dormant for many years, but it comes alive, we do not lose it by distance but may become deaf to its voice if not taught to listen.

If we understand that our body carries our country, we can defeat the victim mentality; people say that if we are not on country, we are not at home and are not therefore real. We can come to believe that because we are off country, our responsibilities to it are no more. As I indicated in my comments about work, this is far from the truth.

Being off country and carrying the country in your body because you were born out of it means you are to live as if you are still there. The work continues. Granted this can be difficult, especially if you are off country not of your own choice. Our responsibility is to fulfil our roles wherever we are and despite any obstacles standing in our way. The ancient spirits note desire and intention, and they will offer support in whatever we attempt to do. Understanding this means we are not victims because we have not ceded our sovereignty as a person or as Wiradjuri.

Our task off country is to walk the country we carry with us and listen, hear and think; reconnect with the song-lines and the 'old people' all around us and remain "who we were before we were born". 'Who we were before we were born' carries with it the sense of continuation, lineage, belonging, beyond ourselves. We are more than our body, and we bring all it entails with us at birth. Here is a sense of always being and – in my experience – that is how it feels. I am in and of this place because I could be of no other. It is not predestination but the knowledge that I have been this place for beyond time, not linear time but unhurried, wandering, 'everywhere, when' time.

"I am a non-resident of (my Aboriginal) country' and 'Even though I am not living there, I belong to (XX)".[62]

---

62 Arabena, K. (2015). *Indigenous to the Universe.* Melbourne: Australian Scholarly Publishing, p. 101

The land owns us

Today, much is made of sovereignty. We often say there is no one pan-Aboriginal nation. We also say there are many Aboriginal nations based around language and dialect groups across this country. We deem these nations to be sovereign, independent and autonomous.

Why? Because this nation was 'settled' under *Terra Nullius* and no first sovereign nation ceded their lands to settlers who came here. The colonisers did not attempt to negotiate with those who were here. Under the *Doctrine of Discovery* and *Terra Nullius*, there was no one here to negotiate with. What some now call the Frontier Wars was simply clearing the vermin from the land.

We often refer to the people in the recognised form of the 'Acknowledgment of Country' as the sovereign custodians or people of a place. It is essential to understand that it is not the people who are sovereign but the land. Not in the sense of a defined and surveyed patch of land. It includes all below, above and roundabout that gives birth and nourishes everything on it, including the people. It is the land that is sovereign because it gives life to all.

The people are sovereign only in the sense of their role to care for and look after the land, including preventing others from taking it from them. They are only sovereign as they carry that land in their body. They are not sovereign owners since the concept of ownership is foreign to indigenous people. There is no word for particular property possession.

The concept of sovereignty is an appropriation of the dominant culture and used only in its legal sense. It speaks of country as clearly defined and agreed upon with sure and firm boundaries. It speaks of sovereignty in terms of laws and rights and entitlements, and while it does pertain to lore, it has no rights and benefits, only responsibilities. These responsibilities are mutual and reciprocal with and for all occupying our space. Our space takes in the land as far as we can see and walk, the air and sky above for as far as we see it and the ground deep beneath our feet. We find sovereignty in the Traditional Story passed down to us which cannot be ceded or shared.

Concepts of ownership and boundaries we hear today – of this belonging to us – are mediated through western overlays on our culture. Country is porous as people always moved into the liminal spaces on the edges for trade and hunting, and have been welcomed and included. Boundaries are not clear cut and are the subject of ongoing negotiation. Strict ownership in the sense of big 'keep out or else" signs was not the norm.

Welcome and collaboration were part of the hospitality required to survive and live in relative harmony with others. The danger of using the word sovereign for which there is no word in our language is that it is both used and understood in its western sense and then becomes a legal term at odds with the practice and spirit of indigenous people.

It is only ours while we maintain the intricate relationship of belonging and the responsibilities that will go with that. It is not ours to exploit. Although our people have indeed done that from time to time, it is not our practice. My father would say, "Look after your land and your land will look after you".

Self-determination

Autonomy comes with country. Country itself is autonomous, and as you carry your country in your body, you are independent. Here is the independence of identity, allowing each piece of country and its people to self-determine their lore, language, kinship and ceremonial practices.

While there are similarities and sometimes shared spaces, each particular country and its people act according to their own sets of traditions as handed down through the ancestors and the elders. While areas are occasionally shared, the culture of the people on which that country primarily stands sets the parametres for action and engagement.

Autonomy to be on sovereign land cannot be ceded to another at any point, and no other will attempt to interfere with the actions of an autonomous people. Again, there may be exceptions, but the general rule is this is our country, and we will conduct our business our way. We will make decisions that suit us.

Sarah Maddison states: *"Being autonomous means making mistakes, being accountable, and fixing those mistakes yourself"*.[63] This is a principle of maturity, a sign that one can live one's life with all the complexities within it and make decisions that are best for you. Being embedded in our country and our lore has always been the Aboriginal way.

The Statement from the Heart[64] is such an important statement because it reveals this to all who read it thoroughly. Twelve initial

---

63 Maddison, S. (2008).
64 Referendumcouncil.org.au. (2020). [online] Available at: https://www.referendumcouncil.org.au/sites/default/files/2017-05/Uluru_Statement_From_The_Heart_0.PDF [Accessed 21 Jan. 2020].

consultations with elders and leaders at twelve different locations were undertaken between December 2016 and May 2017.[65] In this process, people listened, dialogued and agreed. Often, peoples had to relinquish bits and pieces of their autonomy to produce a statement best expressing the desire of the whole. The Statement was the outcome of this generosity. And to have it quashed by the Prime Minister of the time was disrespectful of the work and sacrifice made.

In 2007, the Howard government enacted the Northern Territory Emergency Intervention as a response to the Northern Territory's *AmpeAkelyernemaneMekeMekarle: 'Little Children Are Sacred'*[66] report.

The answer was a punitive and draconian attempt to gain control of communities and to impose a policy-based dependency model on Aboriginal people. The intervention was a neo-colonial response to issues requiring the full complexity of indigenous law to respond to, not the top down, politically-driven ideological response from a paternalistic government.

Maddison writes:

> *Australia's colonial history has created a range of dependencies in Aboriginal communities, against which Indigenous people have struggled in their quest for greater autonomy. Recent debates about the contribution made by 'welfare dependency' to the breakdown of social norms in many communities have paved the way for paternalistic policy that seeks*

---

65 https://www.referendumcouncil.org.au/dialogues.html
66 AmpeAkelyernemaneMekeMekarle: 'Little Children Are Sacred (2019).

to control Aboriginal people's behaviour through coercion and punishment. This article concludes that such policy is precisely the wrong response to problems in Aboriginal communities, as it will further entrench the dependencies that have caused social breakdown in the first place.[67]

Politicians continue to make policies limiting our autonomy – policies such as the cash management card[68] quarantining eighty per cent of your welfare payment and leaving twenty per cent in cash. Not only does this weaken the self-esteem of an already bludgeoned people, it affects local economies and the capacity to model appropriate use of money to our young people. A similar policy is the *Community Development Program (CDP)*, which is a punitive work for the dole scheme that has an unevenly punitive impact on Aboriginal people, particularly in remote areas.[69]

---

67 Maddison, S. (2008). Indigenous autonomy matters: what's wrong with the Australian Government's 'intervention' in Aboriginal communities. *Australian Journal of Human Rights*, 14(1), pp. 41-61.
68 En.wikipedia.org. (2019). *Cashless Welfare Card*. [online] Available at: https://en.wikipedia.org/wiki/Cashless_Welfare_Card [Accessed 12 Sep. 2019].
69 Alicespringsnews.com.au. (2019). *CDP work for the dole scheme gets a hammering – Alice Springs News*. [online]

WIRADJURI DREAMING

Many of the words used to describe Aboriginality have no comparable counterparts in any other language. Dreaming and Dreamtime are two of these. English equates these words to the time of creation as understood traditionally in the creation stories at the beginning of God's self-revelation in the Christian Old Testament Genesis accounts. Interpreted thus, they have a sense of occurring or having been completed in the past.

Such an interpretation is way off the mark.

Understanding Aboriginality is concerned with circles and patterns, concepts such as Dreaming and Dreamtime remain alive and present at the very moment we occupy now. They are the "the everywhere, when"[70] of our interaction with the conscious universe. Creation, new story, comes into being, new interpretations of the story become a part of an ever-evolving tradition.

As Turner suggests, Dreaming is simply the Traditional Story used to explain how what and whom we are on country in our place and space. This Traditional Story is not fixed in telling or in interpretation. Traditional Story does not remain the same but responds to the context and is ever evolving and becoming. Interestingly, there are no words for Dreaming or creation in the Wiradjuri language. It is not an act, or a story told

---

70 Turner, M, McDonald B. and Dobson, V. *Iwenhe Tyerrtye – what it means to be an Aboriginal person*, Alice Springs, N.T. 2010, IAD Press.

against a past event or action now completed, nor is it a far-off dreamlike occurrence. It sits within the liminality of space and time and is elusive to any definition, the western idea of tradition or explanation.

The Dreaming acts in life as the innate story present in country, all we share our country with, and what contains us every day. It is not possible to devise a definition that nails down this concept. It just is. It moves in the air, shimmers in the sun, blows in the wind, rests in the soil, flutters in the trees and butterflies, leaps with kangaroos and wallabies and flows in the rivers. It is why the concept of deep thinking or listening, as described in words from every language is a pivotal Aboriginal posture. If you do not listen, hear and reflect, you will miss it altogether.

I cannot show you Dreaming; just stories, metaphors and myths that open a window on embedded culture and practice. Single examples are simply that and may satisfy Western labelling, but it does not expose the emotion, feeling, and passion that surges through a person who is in the Dreaming. The concepts and ideas involved in this philosophy are not and cannot be translated and explained to the Western mind. To understand, one has to spend time with those who are imbued by the Dreaming. It requires you to be quiet and listen with all your senses to what is happening. While this may sound like black magic (little joke!), it's not, it is the embodying of Aboriginality.

People often speak of dreaming and creation as the same. They are not the same but intricately connected; one without the other results in a life without depth and possibility. The Traditional Story or Dreaming is the air in which we breathe; creation is the space in which we dream. Separately, they are but saplings with the potential of becoming; together, they are the habitat of life.

There are as many creation stories as there are Aboriginal nations. Common is the idea that creatures came upon the earth and after a range of struggles created the land and the people. A common form is the Rainbow serpent. Again, it is more complicated and different creatures are responsible for various landforms and shapes. In our culture, gugaa the goanna is said to be responsible for finding where the hidden water was in a drought and on setting it free to create the Murrumbidgee River, one of the three rivers of Wiradjuri or three rivers country.

Again, creation stories are complex and arise out of the need to make meaning and give meaning to existence. It is how the world we live in has cooperated and participated in the becoming of our lived environment. As noted, the stories tell of animals (balugan), fauna, rivers (bila), fire (guying), water (galling, guugu) and people (mayiny) who have participated in the creation of our country, which cooperates by giving and maintaining life.

The Dreaming or the process of a turnaround as discussed by Yunkaporta is the ongoing evolution of country in which we partake as willing co-creators in our role as custodians. We collaborate with the ancient spirits alive in the world and present everywhere at once. Sometimes these spirits are benevolent and work alongside us; sometimes they are malevolent, working against us towards transformation and renewal. The Dreaming is not always a comfortable place as it challenges us to listen, hear, think and respond in ways that both satisfy the spirits of the ancient people and the needs we are facing.

It can be argued that Aboriginal performative art, including what is now better described as contemporary Australian art, has adapted to the settler overlays and reframed Traditional Story for a new audience, even a new audience of Aboriginal people. This new Aboriginal audience is one extensively distanced from traditions of which many have no personal experience. If some 70-80 per cent of Aboriginal people no longer live in traditional environments underpinned by Traditional Story and practice, it follows that the story they now tell and hear is fundamentally different to that of the pre-settler period. It is radically different because the people and the country are fundamentally different. It is no longer the same as it was.

This change in the means of transmission of story in an oral tradition has changed the story itself; if not the story, then how the traditional story is framed and interpreted, told and retold. The danger is this new adaptation is telling story for the sake of storytelling itself and not for the performative and transformative transmission of meaning-making wisdom. Loss of community life and the processes integral to the passing on of knowledge such as initiation and similar rites, the ways into Traditional Story, have been reduced to isolated and superficial attempts to reconnect with a story spoken about but not experienced.

It then can be argued that much of what we speak of in terms of the Dreaming is significantly different; not in the subject matter or story itself, but in how we hear and experience. This changes Dreaming from an inherent remembering through communal and personal experiential ritual and practice. It is now more that of an archaeologist drawing together bits and pieces one stumbles across, making sense of the past and the present.

For those in urban environments, our understanding is piecemeal and thin. We glean our knowledge from bits and pieces making their way to us through remnants of story told by elders, ethnographers, researchers and anthropologists who researched our people before they lost the spaces of limited sanctuary in the early years. They are incomplete and the nuance and reality of their meaning – like that of language – can only be guessed at and recreated from a distance, a distance that has ripped the sacred text apart.

For those who remain within a traditional story life, less than 30 per cent of whom are chiefly central and northern Aboriginal peoples, the Dreaming remains, on the surface at least, intact. Again, it can be argued these stories have changed, not in content, but in the meaning they have for changed circumstances in a world foreign to the time in which they began their journey. They transmit understandings of the world and the sense of being human on country interpreted as a superstructure underpinning a life under threat from destruction, destruction from which those in the east of the land have never recovered.

It can be argued that much of what is now understood as the Dreaming comes to us through the eyes of those who are not Aboriginal. Aboriginal performative art is now a commercial product. It becomes a means of pleasure and enjoyment for those wishing to buy or possess remnants of a people and their culture. This occurs through the appropriation of performance, writing and art, as people want to have some "traditional story" for themselves. It's rarely seen as an expression of the deep story of a complex and sophisticated society. Instead, it is understood as further evidence of the exotic hunter and gatherer who are valued for their quaintness.

Aboriginal Traditional Story has been reduced to single-story texts for children about frogs, goannas and honey ants, beautiful stories in wonderfully illustrated books reducing the incredible complexity of these stories to a bedtime story read in a comfortable western home. It finds life as art pieces called "My Country" or something similar and purchased for how it sits on our lounge room wall or completes our art collection and not for the real meaning hidden under the many layers of story therein. It finds expression as a staple 'ceremony' for tourists and other consumers through dance and didge[71] performances under the stars, at sporting events and the opening of an event.

All of these celebrate not the deep meaning-making culture but the continuing neo-colonial project of difference, exotic and primitive; to be smiled at and applauded but not a voice one takes seriously. Under this project, commenced with the arrival of the British, the Dreaming or Traditional Story is no longer a living story but is a story of the past with little or no value to those alive today. The people whose story this was have been reduced to a people to be pitied and amused, counted and collated, managed and controlled, and their stories of meaning parked aside in the archives and annals of researchers, academics and entertainment. At the same time, politicians and governments continue to rape and pillage a culture as old as time itself.

Yet the Dreaming adapts and maintains its people for it is not in books or intellectual knowledge, it is embedded in the body of every person who carries our blood, no matter how much. The power of being Aboriginal is not known in the volume of blood but presence. The idea of amount or percentage is a settler's way

---

71   Didgeridoo

of breaking apart and separating kin from each other. It is not how we understand it.

This embedded-ness responds to the urging of the Dreaming heard through story, kinship, walking on country, connecting with familiar totems and totemic experiences and through every breath of the air we breathe holding the spirits empowering life. It is not only a conscious experience. It happens within and around us, and we become aware of who we are, what we need to do and how to do it, and it defies the attempts by others to extinguish its flickering flame coming to life in our "big brain".[72]

In many ways, the Dreaming cannot be either defined or contained. It is beyond the beyond and finds its form appropriate for every age, circumstance and person. It maintains our culture and lore for communal wholeness and balance, not for continuity of an ancient practise or ritual. It is all about being Aboriginal in the time and space we find ourselves.

---

72 Yunkaporta

REPOSITORY OF SACRED TEXTS

Sitting around a fire in the Wominjeka Garden, I speak of country to a group of cub scouts. All the time, I am running dirt gathered for me by a friend through my fingers. At the appropriate moment, I ask them to hold out their hands, and I move slowly around dropping some dirt into the hands and say, "Everything you need to know is here". They receive it as a sacrament, or a sacred ritual would be, and it is. At another time, a 9-year old girl said, "You know what I am going to do? I am going to take this home to my grandfather and grandmother who are from Italy I will put this in their hands and say this is now your country".[73]

The country, in this sense, holds within itself the wisdom laid down over the ages and passed on in traditions daily. Each informs the way the various systems work to resolve the issues communities face.

Country is the space in which we live and is bordered by the horizons all around, the canopy of blue going away above your head and the deep layers or strata of history layered down beneath your feet. It is not a surveyed space delineated from other areas by a fixed dark black line on a paper map.

Within this liminal and porous space, we find our meaning as citizens of the universe and our vocation as custodians of all we can see, hear and feel. Here, we are invested with the knowledge

---

73 Recently, I have formalised this ritual by placing the dirt in a plastic screw-top vial they take home and place on their bedside table so they will always remember the importance of country.

and wisdom to be and do by each breath and interaction with it and those we share it with. Our vocation is to maintain it and the Dreaming it shares with us from our first tree to our last. We have no other purpose.

When we are off country with no hope of return, the working of ancient traditions in law, ceremonial, language and kinship systems begin to break down. The connection, knowledge, is lost, resulting in dysfunction, violence and destruction.

Like the Dreaming I wrote of before, this trauma finds ways to disrupt and reside in us when we are no longer at home. While this is destructive at one level, it is the other side of our vocation now we are no longer on country. Our mission includes our need to reconcile the trauma others have lived before us, and we have lived ourselves. We are responsible for replacing this trauma – some refer to as cross-generational trauma – and building hope and possibility where there was and is pain and violence.

Violence is not foreign to traditional people. They lived in a violent world where when things went wrong, they went catastrophically wrong. Violence within communities was out in the open, measured and controlled and often used as part of sorting out conflict under the law, but it was still violence.

The type of violence present when people are disconnected from the sacred or traditional practices becomes lateral and personal abuse. Violence experienced out of a sense of powerlessness and having no place to call country. Individual disorders like alcoholism, drugs, self-harm and suicide, for example, abound in these communities. Lateral violence against another in the community, domestic violence and more erupt because people are removed from the protection of place and traditional story.

The best defence against this type of violence is to be able to live within communities healthy in tradition and with an understanding that full practice of these traditions is the only, or primary work. It needs to be valued not only by those in the community but by those who seek to make our people become productive consumers. It is not our way. Try living an entirely traditional way of life with all the responsibilities that go with it, and you won't have time to change a tyre!

Traditional story sits within the repository of the sacred text, the ground beneath us and the world around us. It is difficult for those who have law and truth written down in books and entrusted to those responsible for the proper interpretation and implementation of that law to understand what it means to have no connection whatsoever to the source of Traditional Story. This disconnection from the repository, country is often seen as moral or social failure resulting in addiction and destructive behaviours. There is no resolution by punishment or western medicalisation. The only way to treat it is by being reconnected to country.

Kinship

Kinship comes out of the country itself, it comes from the Ancestor Beings, Aboriginal people have grown up deep inside this from Creation, and they live within it always and forever.[74]

In its purest form, kinship explains whom I am responsible to and who is responsible to me. Turner writes that kinship holds

---
74 Turner, M., McDonald, B. and Dobson, V. (2010), p. 76.

people close together, guides and cares for all the generations of people that have "lived within the cradle of the Land", and comes out of the country, our Ancestor itself. In this sense, respect is integral to understanding kinship, and it begins with respect for the Land.

Growing up, we were taught by Dad to walk behind him and to walk in the steps or footprints of the person in front. That way, we did not create more damage to the soil than necessary. Fortunately, my father wasn't a big man, and it was reasonably easy to do!

Looking from the outside (for this fella from the side) it is, as they say in Alice Springs, complicated. Kinship is our roots; it shows how we are to relate to country and how to marry into the right skin groups to ensure country remains as it was from the beginning.

Kinship is all about respect. It explains how individuals relate, who can talk to whom, how to act in front of others and more. There are strict rules on behaviour and interactions, which, if broken, are managed by recourse to traditional laws. It covers boy-girl relationships, marriage, children and more. To fully understand this more, I recommend reading *Iwenhetyerrtye* by M. K. Turner.

Dixon comments:

> Kinship systems – right across the continent – demonstrate the mental agility of the original inhabitants of Australia. But this is not a mind game. Each kin relationship carries important

social obligations. One kin category may have the responsibility for organising a youth's initiation, another for performing the operation. Certain relations are involved in arranging a marriage. When a person dies, mortuary rites are to be organised by a specific relative.[75]

As someone who is not part of a community or a practising kinship group, it is not up to me to write too deeply about it. I do suggest that if you are working with indigenous communities, take the time and be patient in learning the rules where you are so as not to blunder innocently into a disaster.

If we understand that all creatures and things are sentient, then we are in a kinship or network relationship with all. We owe them respect, care and our partnership in maintaining the whole. They too have a mutual responsibility for us. In all kinship relationships, reciprocity is a key ingredient. It is not about one being better, more deserving or entitled than another. Once that happens, it all gets out of whack and goes to custard as they say.

It is the issue humanity faces with climate change and the impact of environmental vandalism. This is predicated on greed, of one group of people believing they are more deserving and have the right to plunder creatures and creation. The present situation of catastrophic weather events in Australia and across the world is testament to this.

One of the five features of indigenous people's relationships to their world is:

---

75 Dixon, R. (2019). *Australia's Original Languages - An Introduction.* 1st ed. Sydney: Allen & Unwin. p. 60

> *Networks of kinship, alliance and animated exchange are founded on a principle that everything is imbued with the same life energy. We are all related because of the singular experience of life in all of us.*[76]

Totems are a significant form of kinship and play an essential role in the kinship system, particularly for Aboriginality being universe referent. It relies on the recognition of the interconnection between all. Totems reflect identity represented by non-human symbols of tribal character; relationship – as both the human and non-human share the essence of creation and are related; worldview – as sharing the philosophy of belonging to one another as the basis of all life in this place.[77]

In other words, totems signify the intricate web of belonging within communities in a specific time and place. They remind us of the respect required to be accorded to each element simply because we share this space and place and are integrally responsible for each other.

Kinship, while more complicated than I have the space to reflect upon here, is more than just a set of community rules for the interaction of people. Kinship relates to how we live our lives in relationship with the whole. It has universal as well as particular implications and draws people into a work that is fulltime and requiring wisdom and skill. This is the work of maintaining all that sustains us. While it does not fit the modernist model of

---

76 Arabena, K. (2015). *Indigenous to the universe*. Melbourne: Australian Scholarly Publishing, pp. 30-31

77 Rose, D. (2019). [online] Environment.nsw.gov.au. Available at: https://www.environment.nsw.gov.au/-/media/OEH/Corporate-Site/Documents/Aboriginal-cultural-heritage/indigenous-kinship-with-the-natural-world-new-south-wales.pdf [Accessed 18 Sep. 2019].

productive work, it is a vocation of responsibility one undertakes on behalf of one's country.

Lore/Law

Lore is the ancient traditions, the law and rituals implicit in the life of the group. Lore or wisdom sets down the parametres for the regulation of community life, what is allowed and what is not, who can do and who can't, marriage and relationship rules, rules regulating punishment for indiscretions against the lore and more. It is not the law as we understand it in western culture, which is an outside body adjudicating on issues from a supposedly discrete distance.

Lore operates democratically within community, allowing all to participate where necessary. Such a process ensures the health of the community over and above the rights of the individual. It is once again complicated, but if you grow up with it, like driving on the left side of the road, it becomes the norm.

Yet it is no more complicated than any other set of community protocols or the law. Explaining western law and cultural norms to a non-westerner will bring about many shakes of the head, some giggles and a lot of complete blankness on both the faces and minds of those listening.

Our bewilderment should not prevent us from making an effort to listen, hear and reflect on what is the way it is in another culture. Lies have been told about Aboriginal lore and law, based in the racist need to eradicate humanity and capacity from non-white people.

Remember, our skin may be black – maybe not as black as you would like – but we are not dumb or stupid. Our culture has never been dumb or stupid either because of its innate sense of the spirit of the universe, the voices of ancestors, human and non-human and its practical need to arrange a complex society to survive and flourish as we did for sixty-five thousand years.

An example of what this looks like is the following from the Noongar people:

> Noongar people have complex lore and customs pre-dating European contact. Our lore has existed alongside European laws and still does today. The terms 'lore' and 'law' are sometimes used interchangeably, but 'law' refers to written European law. Lore for Noongar people is unwritten and refers to kaartdijin (knowledge), beliefs, rules or customs. Noongar lore is linked to kinship and mutual obligation, sharing and reciprocity. Our lore and customs relate to marriage and trade, access, usage and custodianship of land. Traditionally, it has governed our use of fire, hunting and gathering, and our behaviour regarding family and community. Noongar lore works with nature to protect animals and our environment. Noongar people do not eat animals that have totemic significance with our names. This contributes to assuring biodiversity is maintained and food supplies are always in abundance.[78]

---

78 Lore, N. (2019). *Noongar Lore | Kaartdijin Noongar*. [online] Noongarculture.org.au. Available at: https://www.noongarculture.org.au/noongar-lore/ [Accessed 11 Sep. 2019].

Repository of Sacred Texts

In an oral tradition, knowledge is not written down and is passed to those coming after by elders and knowledge keepers. This knowledge refers to beliefs, philosophies, relationships and ritual practice. While not written in the western sense, art and ritual dance and music can be 'read' as a means of transferring knowledge.

Lore is all-encompassing and impacts on the way a people responsible for a parcel of country and each other regulate their storytelling and intra-relationships. It does extend beyond the human and the immediate. It is about designing, communicating and policing all the various ways interactions occur so that all are treated with respect.

Lore is not restricted to us but includes all people who now live on country. This is one of the reasons why an acknowledgment of country is essential. It acknowledges where you are and on whose land you find yourself. It places you both under the protection and hospitality of the local custodians, and it also calls upon you to behave responsibly and be accountable to local lore and practice.

Until we enshrine joint sovereignty, those who came here with and after Captain Philip are responsible to the local lore. The inability to resolve this contributes to the ongoing destruction of the environment and depletion of bio-diversity. The land doesn't forget who has raped her. Until this rift is resolved, the situation will only worsen. It is the way of reciprocity and wholeness, and without reconciliation, there is no resolution.

By the way, we do not eat our totems either. I am reliably told that to cook wagaan (crow), you place it in a fire-pit wrapped in leaves with two reasonable size rocks. After an hour or when the stones are soft, you take it out. You throw away the crow and eat the rocks!

Language

Margaret Kemarre Turner writes, "*The Land needs words. Otherwise, if we didn't have language to speak with, we would only have the thoughts that are inside our heads*". Thoughts are orphans without words. Songs need words. "*So the Land needs words.*"[79]

"*Words make things happen. Words make us alive, the language keeps us alive.*"[80] Words are creative; they are essential to bringing into being the spirit of the land and ensuring the traditions of the ancestors remain and are transferred to future generations.

Turner continues, "*It's not only words that's sacred but also it comes from our own land, and from our ancestors.*" It is a gift to people and the landscape, flora and fauna who have life because of language coming from the land.

Language and the capacity to name connect all as one. Language is not particular in that only humans communicate with other humans. Language crosses species because they all are citizens of the land and universe.

Everything's got a name for it, even ant. Every bird talks different languages, and comes from trees from

---

79 Turner, M., McDonald, B. and Dobson, V. (2010). *Iwenhetyerrtye*. Alice Springs, N.T.: IAD Press. p. 194
80 Turner, M., McDonald, B. and Dobson, V. (2010). *Iwenhetyerrtye*. Alice Springs, N.T.: IAD Press. p. 194.

> our land. All the time we relate to the birds' words and birds' message as well as our own language.[81]

It is specific and practical, relating to what is and grounded in what is. Dixon suggests that languages, including indigenous languages, " – *provide (ing) identity, description, the means for interactions, and a conduit for aesthetic release*".[82] While there are similarities between language groups, even those next door are distinct in crucial ways, reflecting the space and time in which those people developed their languages.

There is no one Aboriginal language. Some suggest we sing the national anthem in an indigenous language as people do in South Africa – try sorting out which one from the 250 plus language groups and at least as many dialects!

In another place, Dixon reminds us that just because Aboriginal people were not as complex in the eyes of western people that their language was simple. He says,

> *People who do not over-exploit the material side of things tend to specialise in those other facets of humankind, the social and the mental. This last is channelled into original languages, which are vehicles for detailed grammatical specification, for the classification of everything around, and for delicate aesthetic expression.*[83]

---

81 Turner, M., McDonald, B. and Dobson, V. (2010), p. 194.
82 Dixon, R. (2019). *Australia's Original Languages - An Introduction*. 1st ed. Sydney: Allen & Unwin. p. 31.
83 Dixon. R. (2009) p. 46.

As one making tentative efforts to learn Wiradjiru, it is indeed complex and complicated and needs much patience and often more brainpower than my ancient brain can muster sometimes.

Language is connected to action and is as concise or as convoluted as the situation requires. A simple no can mean no as English defines it, but it can also mean many variations on this theme – no now, no before, no later, no as response and much more. We do not elaborate – something people may think it is rude, yet it is merely how our language works. If you ask a question in which a simple yes or no is the correct answer, then that is what you will get. There will be 'no thank you' or 'yes that would be nice'. Yes or no may well be what is appropriate in our culture.

Language is also not just the words you use. It is the way you say it, the body language you use, the tone, and who you are addressing. Language is complex and integral to Aboriginality and particular communal identity. It is evidence of the sophistication of our culture before the arrival of the settlers.

Ceremony/Rituals/Story

It is all about story. Ceremony, rituals and knowledge transfer relies heavily on story, whether that story is sung in art, music, song, dance, pictures in the sand or on rock walls or message sticks, clap sticks, boomerangs, shields or didgeridoos. Stories are told and retold to convey the same, same but different and, sometimes, a very different yarn for an ever-changing range of purposes.

Storytellers tell stories with special permission to unlock the hidden stories beneath the surface story. A story is told like a book is read, in one place. You just need to know or have permission to unlock the undisclosed stories. There is always another page or chapter, sometimes a sequel, all wrapped up and hidden in the object or spoken word.

Stories in the oral tradition are both the performative and transformative transmission of all that is needed to be Aboriginal every day. It is in and through the singing and hearing of story found in music, dance and art, that you are opened up to the wisdom layered around you in ordinary everyday experiences.

Telling stories can take place around a fire, or just about anywhere people are yarning. Sometimes they are shared via a drawing in the sand or dirt without words but told all the same. These stories transfer knowledge if you listen carefully and allow the patterns to unfold.

All ceremonies and rituals are story-based. Dance, music, song, poetry are not free form. They follow a pattern and tell a particular story. It has a purpose needing to unfold as per tradition. Most cultures, for example, have specific styles or types of language and structure for a song they may sing for a particular purpose.[84] It isn't random. It follows a pattern and makes use of specific words and phrases.

I watched my father tell stories with a stick in the sand. Sometimes they were stories we had heard before only their meaning was different. We would challenge him. He would smile and reply, "Same story, different meaning".

---

84 Dixon, R. (2019). *Australia's Original Languages - An Introduction.* 1st ed. Sydney: Allen & Unwin.

Rituals, even the more accessible such as Welcome to Country, smoking ceremonies for a range of purposes and similar, all have layers of story and meaning. They are contextual and respond to a place, people and circumstances. Each time they are carried out, they are responding to the moment and are unique and particular. They are not repeatable in the sense that the same words are preordained. The meaning remains. The process is always different.

Rituals and ceremonies are founded in the deep-rooted Traditional or Dreaming stories providing the superstructure for life. These stories are similar and sometimes shared but are particularised and stratified according to place, space and time. They are also personalised by those who are doing the telling and the reasons why they are. Stories are not heard and intellectualised but read and performed. Transformation takes place in the "big brain" the gut, the home of emotion and feeling; the place where all action and response occurs.

Interestingly, many of these stories, when told to non-indigenous audiences elicit an emotional and performative response, especially with children. These stories do not resonate with rational thought responses but with a deep emotional or personal response. Children understand what it was like for Tiddalick the frog, Gugaa the goanna or Dirawan the emu.[85] They have been there. They get it in their big brain. Adults only respond with their little brain.

---

85 Carthew, M. and Rogers, G. (2007). *Tiddalick the thirsty frog*. London: Collins

THE ROCKS SPEAK

Country is not passive. It is alive with the energy of the universe and those who have lived out of and returned to it. It speaks and acts primarily to those who walk it and listen to hear what it is saying by its actions and its words. The four primary elements – water, wind, earth, fire – map the visible language but as we understand all things to be sentient even the most unlikely aspect will speak, as my father said, "Walk your country and listen closely. If you do, it will tell you what it needs and what you need to do". And it does.

Tyson Yunkaporta tells the following story in his book *Sand Talk* to illustrate:

> For a long time, tourists took stones away from that sacred site (Uluru) as souvenirs, then a few decades ago something strange began to happen. The tourists started mailing the rocks back with panicked reports of weird happenings, disturbed sleep, bad luck, ghostly visitations and terrible accidents. Somehow they knew it was because of the rocks, and were sending them back with desperate apologies. So many were returned that they had to build a big storage shed to house them.
>
> In our Law we know that rocks are sentient and contain spirit. You just can't pick one up and carry it home, as you will disturb its spirit and it will disturb you in turn. (....) A lot of rocks are benevolent and

enjoy being used and traded, but you have to know which ones you can use. Rocks are to be respected.[86]

All of creation is alive with spirit, aware of kinship in all its forms and able to interact with all surrounding it. Humanity has no more call on superiority than anything else. All share the same energising spirit of life and being, and therefore all are indelibly connected. Each is kin of the other and required to live out the custodial ethic in terms of responsibility and reciprocity. Here is the premise of Arabena's book[87] and all traditional Aboriginal thinking (Dreaming).

The land, as a sentient being has memory. A bizarre statement to some but it does remember and responds out of that memory. It remembers who it is – our mother – and lives that role by offering to us all the elements we need for an abundantly enough living. It recognises its capacity and can only give as much as it can. It can provide no more. It remembers what gives it life and what it needs to be alive for all others. If we deny this through bad management, a 'greater than' attitude by those who occupy her or reduce her to a commodity and not kin, she will simply not do what is required or what we deign she should do.

Like all relationships, our relationship with the land and all it holds requires our devotion, time and listening. No human relationship thrives if it does not get the time necessary to develop and deepen. No skill can develop without time, listening and practice. For Aboriginal people, these are the elements building up the relationship with their particular country over many

---

86 Yunkaporta, T. *Sand Talk*. 2019, 1st ed. Melbourne, Vic.: Harper One, pp. 40-41.
87 Arabena, K. (2015). *Indigenous to the universe*. Melbourne: Australian Scholarly Publishing, pp. xiii-xiv.

thousands of years. The methods we speak about here weren't part of some technological project. The rudimentary technology necessary was developed for and of the relationship already in train. The failure of current land use is the ignorance of memory and connection. Ours is one of the land being a commodity required to fulfil our plans and requirements. It has no agency and has no time to develop a voice; a voice Aboriginal people listened for innately.

All Aboriginal land practice and human relationships have their beginning in these philosophical underpinnings. The idea that all of creation consists of the same elements. It, therefore, requires an equivalency or a corresponding level of respect and reverence as one's self is integral in a society where possessions and power do not have primacy and where time is taken to recognise patterns of belonging.

It is a philosophy that loathes the idea of continual growth and development. As noted above, Aboriginal technological development occurred to solve particular problems, not to create more. It is a philosophy of enough, enough not as a deficit but as sufficient. Enough meets our needs and doesn't result in greed, waste and the need for property, carts to carry possessions or jealousy amongst the people. Enough for us means that there is also enough for the other – animals, soil, plants, birds, fishes and more. We leave in the ground sufficient not just for the time the land lies fallow and regenerates but for the allotted time when we will return and require the land to sustain us again. A philosophy of perpetual growth never occurred to us because that would have meant taking what belonged to others, and that was against the law.

In terms of land and resource management, this empowers a sense of responsibility and reciprocity. It ensures that we take deliberate care to ensure there is always enough for those who are the means for sustenance and survival. The land and animals are not overused or over farmed, to ensure they flourish individually, enjoying all they need to contribute to the intricate interconnection necessary for survival. Bio-diversity is maintained, ensuring each has what it needs. It is all about wholeness and balance, continuing the circle of life.

In the recent devastating bushfires in Australia, much was made of cultural or cool burning, a custodial practice carried out by Aboriginal people to clear, 'cultivate' and regenerate areas required for the maintenance of theirs and others life. While I applaud the interest in cultural burning, there are some crucial things to remember:

- Cultural burning works on small-scale burns and was used as part of a long term practice to create appropriate spaces for grazing and safety over time.
- It was not a broad scale practice such as in wilderness areas, i.e. wild bush, mountain areas, etc.
- It is labour intensive and to burn on a large scale requires vast numbers of people.
- It was carried on in native or indigenous vegetation and not on the very different landscape we now have with introduced species being the prominent vegetation.
- It ensured bio-diversity by allowing natural vegetation to regenerate and native creatures to have access to the resources they required to thrive.

- It supported a form of rotational farming. After an area had been used in the appropriate season and burnt, the people moved to the next space. It was thus allowing the area up to 12-18 months regeneration before it was required to support them on their return. Interestingly, this length of time is one that occurs in the work of regenerative farmers like David Marsh.
- This practice took place in a culture that did not prioritise property. The bush was free of buildings, stock and fences, which would burn if a burn escaped — escape they did.
- Devastating bushfires did still occur in those areas where people did not deem it appropriate to burn, mountainous bush areas, for example. Here the fires were allowed to burn out because there was no property to protect. People just moved.

Life followed a different set of seasons than the four we now have. In Wiradjuri culture, there are the following:

> *Cool to warming weather*: *with rising river levels filling up billabongs, lakes and creeks, and land animals moving off flood plains in preparation for flooding, the increasing water would see an increase in the population of food sources such as: kangaroos, emus, small animals such as lizards, possums, wombats, fish, mussels, yabbies, bird eggs, witchetty grubs and water birds.*
>
> *Hot and dry weather*: *With water levels declining, fish traps where made and restored because of receding*

water. People would stay near the water i.e. swamps, billabongs and rivers which would provide a rich diet of: fish, crayfish, mussels, water birds.

Cold to freezing weather: With many animals hibernating, they had to be dug out which took a lot of effort and time. With people moving away from the rivers because it was too cold and foggy. The hunting of game that also provided skins for warmth such as: wombats, echidna, snake, possum, kangaroo and in some areas koalas.

Cool to warm weather: With the rivers and water levels becoming very low, animals return to the water holes and rivers because there was not a lot of vegetation on the plains: wombats, echidnas, snakes, lizards, emus, possums, kangaroo and, in some areas, koalas.[88]

Growing up, I learnt about the Wiradjuri supermarket – the kurrajong tree. On the farm, my father ensured that these trees remained when land clearing occurred. Often they were solitary and obvious, sitting out from everything else and occupying a visible and discernible landscape they appeared to own. And own it they did.

Kurrajong (Brachychiton species), the yellow seeds can be roasted and eaten. Fibre from the inner bark can be used for fishing lines and nets. The roots can be tapped in times of drought for water. Kurrajong seeds comprise 18% protein and 25% fat and yield high

---

88 https://wiradjuriculture.com.au/food-dhangaang/

levels of zinc and magnesium. Inner bark crushed in water and the liquid used as an eyewash (Stewart & Percival 1997).

Food was prepared in a variety of different ways. Seeds and nuts were ground up using a grinding or, if necessary, the seeds were soaked or leached in water for days in order to make them edible. Water was added to the powder and the mixture was kneaded into dough. The dough could then be eaten or cooked.[89]

My father used this tree to sustain stock in the worst of droughts. He would say you do not carry more stock than your land can carry in the worst of conditions. He was faithful to that rule and never had to bring in outside hay or grain to feed stock. He had trees, kurrajong trees in particular. The leaves provided both nutrients and water sufficient to meet the needs of thirsty sheep. He would selectively lop each tree in a way that meant the tree itself regenerated and flourished and was always able to assist the stock when required.

My father farmed in the ancient way, conscious of the interrelationship between all created elements. He used Wiradjuri "conservation techniques to ensure the continued supply of foods, maintain the environment and ensure the survival of species are key elements for both agricultural and aquaculture practices. From the practice of removing several bird eggs (not all) from a nest to more complex fire management and seasonal food calendars, he and his people ensured survival not only of themselves but of the natural environment."[90]

---

89 https://wiradjuriculture.com.au/food-dhangaang/
90 https://wiradjuriculture.com.au/food-dhangaang/

Was this a learnt practice for him, or was it a part of his relationship with the land? Perhaps it was a bit of both but allowed him to weather droughts, fires, floods and more with destruction occurring on his farm. I do not remember him losing stock during droughts because of his land management. He was the living out of his custodial ethic of responsibility and reciprocity based on the idea of "if you look after the land, it will look after you".

I heard it often.

UNIVERSE AS COUNTRY

Aboriginal life is not about the particular as the solitary place of meaning. It is referent to the universe – to what is above, what is below, and what is 'round-about'. It is for wholeness, balance and all my cousins.

> *Kelly Arabena in her work,* Becoming Indigenous to the Universe, *reminds us that we are indigenous to the whole, our responsibility is connected directly to our kinship to all, and it is only when we remove ourselves solely from being indigenous to our particular place and identity do we find a way to live in kinship with the beating heart of our mother, this planet, and our cousins, every single grain of dirt, leaf, droplet of water, breath of air and living creatures. It is only when we are able to mourn the loss of the least of these as the deepest personal loss can we begin to understand our predicament and begin to resolve the issues we face.*[91]

Indigenous people have always been indigenous to the whole. They are universe referent in that they look out, up and down to include all in their kinship and traditional life. They practise inclusion, not entirely but with intent. Elizabeth Johnson in *Ask the Beasts* reminds us we need to move from an anthropocentric focus to look toward the heavens.[92]

---

91 Loughrey, G. (2019). *Living the Change (Australian Religious Response to Climate Change).*
92 Johnson, E. (2015). *Ask the beasts.* London: Bloomsbury.

The period in which we are living has become known as the "Anthropocene" from *anthropo* (human) and *cene* (new) – because humankind has caused mass extinctions of plant and animal species, polluted the oceans and altered the atmosphere, among other lasting impacts.[93] Will Steffen from Australia National University's Climate Change Institute states, the name is "another strong reminder to the general public that we (humans) are now having undeniable impacts on the environment as a whole, so much so that a new geological epoch has begun".

Johnson's suggestion encompasses the natural perspective of the original people. We are not in this alone, and we do not have the primacy of knowledge over what is and what the universe itself needs. We remain detached in these modern times from any significant connection to country and to what is not human. We preference the capacity of our so-called logical brain, what Aboriginal people call the small brain, over the deep emotional or intuitive listening with all our senses to what we are living amidst through our gut or large brain. Reading the sky and the stars and moon provides deep and vital information necessary for making sense of surviving in our dangerous world.

My father would study the night sky every night, looking for signs of rain or unusual weather and indications of future weather down the way. He would see what the ring around the moon was doing, how many stars if any were in it and be able to predict when rain was coming. He would watch the flight of birds, particularly red-tailed black cockatoos; the activity of ants and the breeding patterns of kangaroos and make more accurate predictions than the weather bureau, both short and long term.

---

[93] Stromberg, J. (2020). What is the Anthropocene and Are We In It? *Smithsonian*, (January 2013).

Universe as Country

The universe is country. Sky (murrumbir) holds within all held within the country beneath it. From it comes wisdom and guidance and is referenced by Aboriginal people for all of life. The piece of sky above us and only touching down on the edges of our horizon hold in place our world and provides us with another resource within the indigenous knowledge system.

What is in the sky is on the ground. Aboriginal people understand that they are the offspring of the universe and the earth and carry the same spirit within them as all other created elements. They are not special because they are human. One with all others, they have the responsibility to engage and partner with nature for the good of all.

This understanding of the universe as the giver and holder of all life is inherent in the custodial ethic that underpins the day-to-day engagement with country. What is a custodial ethic and what does it look like in practice is a key question for the ongoing care of ourselves and all our cousins – those with whom we share this land – animate and inanimate, human and non-human.

For Aboriginal people, relationships between them and the universe in which they live are fixed and unchanging. Our primary contact with the country on which we are born, live and die, defines us. It is a reciprocal relationship in which we understand the web of inter-relationships binding and holding us to each other and to the country itself.

A custodial relationship is not a choice we make. It is the way we understand who we are responsible for and who is responsible for us. It applies in personal and tribal relationships and on the universal level as well. The country cares for us, and we care for the country. It is a reciprocal relationship and allows neither to take more than they need from each other.

It requires us to be in open dialogue with all around us. Country is not only the ground beneath our feet, but all water, trees, rocks, creatures, stars and clouds, etc. within our vision. We are to walk our land and to listen carefully. If we do so, we will hear what it has to say to us, what we need to do and why we need to do it.

On a local level, Aboriginal law lays down the parametres for this open dialogue. Through ceremony, story and totems, we remind ourselves of the relationships forged through the ongoing dreaming we inhabit and to transmit to those in the present and future.

Living a custodial ethic requires us to relinquish our propensity to know better and to control nature. Sitting with the holders of these stories and listening, hearing and reflecting, we will find pathways to a reciprocal relationship with the environment.

If we share the essence of life with all in our world, then we have no priority of existence more significant than any other. We are to treat the contained and the container, the creatures and the universe, with deep respect and equality. We do not take what is "not ours" or more than what is our appropriate share. Land use practices necessary to sustain life occurred in a limited and controlled manner, including clearing, damming, burning. There was no large-scale clearing or burning and particularly none in those areas which would not provide for the maintenance of life such as wild, mountainous areas.

Bushfires did occur in the 'wilder' areas, mountainous and mostly uninhabited, as a result of lightning strikes and wayward burns. When they did occur, these were allowed to burn out in their own time or until the weather changed and put them out. As a people who did not value property and their right to live where they pleased above all other rights, they did not put themselves or others at risk protecting property. The simply moved out of the way.

The way of the universe decreed their country was sovereign, and they responded appropriately. They lived on country in smaller numbers, probably groups of 40 or 50 in most instances and did not place substantial burdens on land and resources. They adapted and moved. Their agricultural methods, where deployed, were designed equally for those they shared the area with and their own needs.

Being indigenous to the universe – Arabena suggests in her book – is the primary learning we can take from the indigenous people. If we live in harmony with the world, recognising that our particular country is part of a much larger country, we begin to understand our place in it. Here is a patchwork of interconnection with country containing the whole of life and existence, understanding it this way allows us to asses and, if necessary, change the way we engage. We will change from an anthropocentric 'greater than' worldview to one of humility and equality. We are reliant on each other, human and non-human, animate and inanimate and therefore will not foul our own nest so to speak.

The universe to the particular; the particular to the universe.

> If there is to be peace in the world,
> There must be peace in the nations.
> If there is to be peace in the nations,
> There must be peace in the cities.
> If there is to be peace in the cities,
> There must be peace between neighbours.
> If there is to be peace between neighbours,
> There must be peace in the home.
> If there is to be peace in the home,
> There must be peace in the heart."
>
> *Lao-Tse*

Here is a simple concept of balance and freedom, giving peace at each particular place in the space we inhabit.

Lao-Tse echoes indigenous thought and Aboriginality in this ancient statement. For indigenous people, life is a circle in which the particular is held and holds within it the very thing it is held by – universal or communal citizenship. *The Statement of the Heart* and its invitation to society finds its rationale in this idea. It is the invitation of a universe referent people and identity who understand their citizenship in this place as reflected in Lao-Tse's statement.

There is no I in our culture without an accompanying us or we. We do not be – alone, for in being we impact the whole. It is how we understand our existence and the purpose of existence. We exist for the all and whatever we achieve or become, we do it, not for ourselves, but for our people.

Aboriginal people are born out of the ground under a tree. The soil, our country contains the sacred text of wisdom laid down over the 65,000 years or more since our people have walked this land. In that sacred text is written all we need to be and what we are responsible for contributing to it. It holds our consolations and trauma, our lives between the trees, the places where we are born, and where we die. We live our lives to leave behind the wisdom we have learnt in our own lives while working to reconcile the trauma we inherit and experience.

It's important to remember all whom we welcome to our land; even those who have committed and continue to commit terrible crimes against us are participants in this story. Born out of this land under a tree (a particular place), you are responsible to what is written and for writing a reconciled future story.

This concept is not ours in exclusivity. We invite you to shift from your embedded way of being and begin the journey with us into joint citizenship in this place. Together we can bring into being an equitable peace, referencing all as equals.

What does this citizenship look like? It is not only citizenship of the immediate, tribe, country or humanity. It is the citizenship of our Father the Universe and of the Earth as our Mother. It is citizenship we share with all our cousins, the mass of created sentient and non-sentient beings who share this universe with us. It is citizenship surging toward wholeness and balance. Both are fundamental indigenous ideas.

Elizabeth Johnson asks, *"Is God's Charity Broad Enough for Bears?"* We think so and think it also includes non-Wiradjuri, non-indigenous, non-human forms.

- To live with an inclusive understanding of citizenship or as indigenous of the Universe (the whole) ensures we leave 'no-thing' out and we work toward peace in each interaction with our kin (our cousins).

- To see ourselves as indigenous of the universe ensures we seek balance as normative, not as the exception. Balance involves the use and distribution of resources, the mediation of power and control for the good of all, and understanding responsibility in place of entitlement and rights.

- To see ourselves as indigenous of the universe ensures that when we are aware of injustices occurring to another in our name, we right the wrong within ourselves and in the particular citizenships we practise. Why? What others experience involves us regardless of whether they are human or non-human. We cannot be at peace if others are out of balance.

- To see ourselves indigenous of the universe implies we are indigenous of place – the universe to the particular to the universe. We are to seek a balance where we are amongst those with whom we share that particular space. Thomas Merton says the reason there is no peace in the world is that the individuals are not at peace with themselves.[94] We must begin in the particular. Merton also says the only journey a human being makes is an inner journey to peace.[95]

- Not to see ourselves as indigenous of the universe implies our inner self is separate from our universe (al) self. It is reasonable to suggest, this is not the case. Jesus referred to himself and his Father as being one. As Jesus, a man of two countries, strove to unite in himself the universe and the particular to bring about

---

94 Merton, T. (2002). *The ascent to truth*. San Diego: Harcourt.
95 Merton, T. (1973). *The Asian journal of Thomas Merton*. [New York]: [New Directions Pub. Corp.], p. 296.

the possibility of peace, so must we. It is where peace begins.

In terms of reconciliation, being indigenous of the universe is exemplified in *The Statement from the Heart*. In the *Statement*, the particular (elders, clans and tribes) sought to bring together a statement reflective of their particular citizenships to deliver a pathway to peace as citizens of the universe.

On the way to this statement, as Bruce Pascoe said, people gave up their hostilities, desires, long-held views, to make the journey from their particular world into the vast and ever-extending world outside. That is why it so powerful.

Its power exists in not being a demand but an invitation to journey from the particular of conflict into the universe of peace – makarrata. The process begins in the immediate particular – being heard and hearing the other (Voice) and when both have heard each other we then move when the time is right, and it may be a long time, to a treaty. We can only 'do treaty' when we hear and have been heard and know it. Then we have a basis to discuss the legal implications in both languages, the language of western law and sovereign nations law.

Once we have a basis for treaty and one has been drawn up, then there is the capacity and the foundation for truth-telling. We cannot do truth-telling until we have a voice, have been heard and have heard the other or until we have agreed about what our relationship will or can be.

Only then can we talk about reconciliation and lastly recognition. To do either of these on a western time-line runs the risk of losing the only thing we have left - our individual, national sovereignties. Once we appear in the constitution, those sovereignties disappear. If we have not achieved voice, treaty and truth-telling before recognition, there is no reason for the other to need to do these things – our sovereignty has been taken away in the superficiality of being recognised.

Remember that as Aboriginal time is circular and the Dreaming is the "everywhere-when", this process does not run in a straight line. The circle continues just like the laying down of layers of wisdom from our lived experiences in our country (sacred text) adds to and changes the story beneath our feet.

So where does that leave us in terms of becoming citizens of the Universe together? If we are waiting for those in power to take us to reconciliation, we are deluding ourselves. They simply do not have the imagination to deal with the issue of sovereignty and legitimacy of the Commonwealth's proclaimed settler sovereignty. It hasn't happened despite the many opportunities there have been to do so.

It can only happen if we, in our own lives, begin to live as indigenous of the universe and take responsibility for peace and reconciliation. This inner journey Merton speaks of will bring us out into a world where we have no other option than to practise reconciliation ourselves. Our vocation is to be the salt of the earth, seasoning through diversity directly from country beneath our feet. We are to become the means of making right what has been and is a great wrong.

I suggest the practice of whina-nga-rra (Wiradjuri) – listen, hear and reflect, taking however long it takes, to understand each other fully.

In this sense, reconciliation only happens when we:

- Learn about what has happened. It really did happen and often was far more traumatic than the writing can tell.
- Read and research the information available in the public domain. There is no excuse for not knowing.
- Listen and don't talk over or back. Don't pretend to know the story.
- Engage with programs in direct partnership with our people. With, not to. We can lead.
- Decide that the cost of giving up entitlement as people in possession of stolen goods is less than the price paid and continues to be paid by our people. The figures are in the public arena, and again, the story is often more terrifying than the numbers.

Finally, find peace with yourself amid this process. Unless you are at peace (not complacent acceptance) with self and circumstances, your actions will be actions motivated by guilt, anger and the desire to fix it, now. That will only make it worse.

We are to approach this with renewed minds, we know what happened, and it was wrong. We are ready to listen and hear how this affected the other and express our remorse. We are willing to walk the journey of *The Statement from the Heart* without reservation, no matter the cost.

Only then will we have peace in particular and in the universe.

LIVING THE CHANGE

I received an invitation to speak at a gathering of the Australian Religious Response to Climate Change group as part of the *Living the Change* campaign. Two of ARRCC's deepest convictions are:

- We believe the Earth is a sacred gift.
- We believe each of us has the responsibility to live in a way that supports and sustains our common home.

"Observations throughout the world make it clear that climate change is occurring, and rigorous scientific research demonstrates that the greenhouse gases emitted by human activities are the primary driver."[96]

While I congratulate *Living the Change* for its two deepest convictions, I have my reservations also. My problem with these two convictions is that they sound anthropocentric – they are about us. In the way they are written, it presumes that the gift is for human beings and that only human beings have a responsibility to and can benefit from action to support and sustain our common home.

Now this concern does not stop with *Living the Change*. The many others I reviewed are all anthropocentric. The cause is human, and the primary reason to resolve this issue is the survival of the human race and our economic system. There is little mention of the voices of non-human sentient beings in this

---

96 Climate Change: Vital Signs of the Planet. (2019). *Scientific Consensus: Earth's Climate is Warming.* [online] Available at: https://climate.nasa.gov/scientific-consensus/ [Accessed 20 Sep. 2019].

discussion. They are the collateral damage in a system focused entirely on us.

Now that may sound an extreme generalisation, and it is. I understand that there are people and organisations with interest in the whole, not the part. Still, the primary focus is on one specific form of citizenship – productive neo-modernism and the human-animal, which benefits primarily from such.

Citizenship in these two statements is about human beings – the citizenship of the human-animal on this planet. Citizenship in our modern times is about the commercial individual, both singularly and communally, to contribute to sustainable growth (an oxymoron) and consumption. We are citizens if we both contribute to sustainable production and consume its products. Our focus is on maintaining the world so it will continue to provide us with what we want from it – resources and hospitality. We want to use it and be sustained by it.

Our language of citizenship or belonging is about people first and foremost. What we need is a new language, which situates us, not as the only citizens of the world, but as one along with all our cousins who constitute creation and are citizens with rights and responsibilities alongside us. These citizens rarely receive an invitation to participate in our conversation and dialogue. We may deign at times to act on their behalf, but it is from our position of prominence and not of equity and shared hopes and dreams.

Writers such as Kerry Arabena and Bruce Pascoe, and theologians such as Elizabeth Johnson, John Haught, Teilhard de Chardin and Matthew Fox are essential reading if we are going to find a way forward. Not just for the human race but the whole of God's sentient creation.

In the 2015 encyclical *Laudato Si*,[97] Pope Francis reminds us of the importance of our role as custodians of creation on behalf of those with whom we share this place. An important idea. If we simply place ourselves as God's appointed caretakers, we run the risk of acting only on our behalf, no matter how good our intentions are. The worse the situation of the planet gets, the more we think only about ourselves.

In his book *Dark Emu*, Bruce Pascoe reminds us what we have lost in the colonial genocide – not only people but a highly sophisticated culture, one that had found its home in this environment and lived within its means. Aboriginal agriculture and land use was adapted to the environment and allowed equal space and time for all to benefit from the vagaries of our country. Genocide not only destroyed practices but destroyed the land and water on which we rely.

It is not enough now to suggest a return to that way of being as the immediate solution. That is romantic nostalgia and simply won't solve all our problems. It will help but not fix. We are to understand pre-modern engagement with the environment had a negative, albeit much smaller, impact on our world. No human activity has been "sinless".

At an environmental conference at Galong in NSW, I stood on the side of the hill with several environmental scientists and

---

[97] W2.vatican.va. (2019). *Laudato si' (24 May 2015)* | *Francis*. [online] Available at: http://w2.vatican.va/content/francesco/en/encyclicals/documents/papa-francesco_20150524_enciclica-laudato-si.html [Accessed 20 Sep. 2019].

surveyed the scene. The scientist next to me pointed across the landscape towards the horizon and said, "Your people would not recognise this as the land they walked on. Only that line of trees (some gums on the creek's edge) would be recognisable. The rest is imported and cultivated. Not even the grass is from here".

The next day, we spent time on one of the farms featured in the ground-breaking book *The Call of the Reed Warbler*[98] and saw the benefit of non-interventional regeneration in agricultural practice. While all the other farms around were bare and showing evidence of erosion, this was lush and alive. Here was the result of 20+ years of renewal and there was more to be done. While it was productive, it was not productive in the manner required to produce more.

Sustainability in place of production was the mantra. My father would say that once farming became a business and not a lifestyle, destruction would follow.

Questions

- Do we have enough time to reform agricultural practices in this country to be in line with traditional worldviews? Do we understand that to do so may well save the environment but not provide the growth required to keep up with the demand for agricultural products?
- Are we able to shift our focus from production to sustainability while the pressure grows to provide sufficient food and other resources?

---

98 Massy, C. (2018). *The Call of the Reed Warbler*. Chelsea Green Publishing.

- Are we willing to let go of the quality of lifestyle and choice we now have to engage with enough? Can our reliance on coal in all its forms to provide us with comfort and warmth be successfully replaced by renewables? The evidence says yes. Others say no, and we say we do not want to lose the level of comfort we already have.

- What is enough and whose enough are we going to settle for? Human beings are creatures of habit, and we have become habitually addicted to having what we want and as much as we want. Australians as a nation are one of the most travelled in the world. We take more regular overseas long haul travel than people from most other countries. Are we able to stay at home and cut our carbon footprint? Can we get used to voluntarily letting go of our "rights" and accepting that to sustain our planet, we have to be satisfied with less?

I fear answering these questions from a modern or 'neo-modern' perspective is beyond us because, in both paradigms, sustainability relates to progress, the concept of more. We need a paradigm shift taking us to a postmodern worldview.

Postmodernity, in terms of colonialism and environmental colonialism, requires both the oppressor and the oppressed coming together to design a new way of seeing and moving forward as partners. In terms of the environment, this means it is not only the human perspective that matters. All affected by our destruction of the environment must be heard and have a say in what happens next. At all levels, this has yet to occur in Australia.

I also fear to answer this from Scripture and theology. The first is always problematic, making Scripture speak in support of your ideas, and, secondly, I am not a theologian, just a bumbling blackfella priest. The Old Testament is replete with a natural theology equating the care of the world as care of God's creation, a theology not out of sync with Aboriginality.

God of the Universe and the natural world appear over and over again in partnership. This same Great Creator Being speaks through valleys, mountains, storms, winds, fires and the seasons. Created beings stand in solidarity with Jesus, our elder in the desert, he appears on the lake in a storm, and he spends much of his time walking his country with his mob. Spiritual truths are similar to mustard seeds, salt, fig trees and birds of the fields.

Somewhere we allowed our capabilities as people – even Christian people – to dominate the non-human in God's Universe. We need communal repentance and transformation of heart and practice.

So what would that look like?

- Seeing ourselves as people with multiple citizenships – local, national, international and of the Universe – with a range of responsibilities requiring alignment to be of benefit to all. It is not about the needs of Australia and Australians but also of Pacific Islanders and their homes, polar bears and disappearing ice-caps and the platypus and their shrinking footprint. These are co-citizens who share this space and time with us and must not be sacrificed to our sense of superiority.

- Recognising the needs of human beings does not trump the needs of those who are unable to have a voice in the dialogue – the environment and creatures who are our cousins. New Zealand Maoris speak this concept except they say "All my relatives" and mean the created world.

- Accepting our responsibility for damaging our mother, the earth, and the universe, our father, and humbly seek new ways of being here, bringing about vital renewal in both spheres. As the statements I read in my research affirmed: we are in this predicament because of our impact on the world. Nobody else is to blame except humans. It then behoves us to accept our responsibility for what has occurred and to take a collaborative lead in bringing about healing.

- Listen to the voices of the world. We have lost the art of winha-ngra-rra (Wiradjuri) – listen, hear and think before doing. We do not do this well. Why? Because we know the answer and how to fix it. Sometimes our "little brains" are a hindrance, not a help. Listen, hear and then give it some time before saying you know what to do.

- Avoid quick and romantic solutions and allow ourselves to respond when we are sure that when we do so, we will not cause more harm. Recycling may seem a good idea, but if we are unable to handle the processing and it all ends in a landfill, what's the purpose? Regenerating the ravaged paddocks with natural grasses sounds excellent, but what do we do while we wait for them to grow?

All this may not seem enough, and it is not, but unless we begin to dialogue with the whole, no one thing will be. It requires us to close the gap down, not up. It's not about sustainable progress. It is about what is enough, just, appropriate for a world and its people living under the genocide of neo-modernism?

Unless we can find our way to that place, no amount of action will make a lot of difference.

PATTERNS EVERYWHERE

The toe bone's connected to the foot bone,
The foot bone's connected to the ankle bone,
The ankle bone's connected to the leg bone,
Now shake dem skeleton bones![99]

Aboriginal people do not just read what is visible but look for patterns of connection and interaction and so interpret how each impacts upon the other. An ancient form of 'if this, then this, and then this' ad infinitum. No-thing acts alone, and there is not one simple linear outcome. No-thing goes in a straight line. No-thing stands alone.

Pattern thinking is the interconnection of life and being and the various patterns of both that intertwine across our country. If we could rise above the earth high enough to see them, song-lines intertwine across our land. I grew up on the top of a song-line – the Great Dividing Range. It is not a divider but a connector, necessary to maintain the patterns of knowledge transfer across this land and between people, just as the Great Barrier Reef is not a barrier but a song-line connecting creation to creation.

Patterns are essential to Aboriginal thinking and philosophy. For example, a deep understanding of patterns gives us many different seasons. Standard calendars are static and set. Yes, the day may differ from year to year, but the four seasons come according to what is on the calendar, not what is happening in the world.

---

99 Songsforteaching.com. (2019). *Dem Bones: Song Lyrics and Sound Clip.* [online] Available at: https://www.songsforteaching.com/folk/dembones.php [Accessed 20 Sep. 2019].

You often hear people say that a season is late or going on beyond when it should have ended. No Aboriginal person would say that seasons come late, because our existence is not linear and not broken into recurring segments. It is unending in its circularity, meaning everything returns but not in the same way.

By being aware of the patterns, the interconnections, the information shared by our country and all we share it with, we know when times are changing and a new season is here. We do not demand it comes when we say it should. We discern patterns that tell us it is here, and we are always on the lookout for the relevant trends to appear.

The patterns are always the same, but every set of patterns is different. No-thing is absolute or set in stone. It is always moving and changing. The patterns are the same – a bird singing or flying in a particular direction, kangaroos giving birth, stars revealing certain formations and more. What are different are how these come together, and what a specific collection of patterns means.

Now I am going to defer to Angie Abdilla to explain pattern thinking further. Writing about a robotics program making use of Indigenous Knowledge Systems, she quotes Vicki Greaves on song-lines:

> *For Aboriginal people, each of the lines represents the law or knowledge that prescribes these connections and provides the blueprint for ensuring that they continue.*[100]

---

[100] Angie Abdilla, R. (2019). *FCJ-209 Indigenous Knowledge Systems and Pattern Thinking: An Expanded Analysis of the First Indigenous Robotics Prototype Workshop*. [online] Twentyeight.fibreculturejournal.org. Available at: http://twentyeight.fibreculturejournal.org/2017/01/23/fcj-

Song-lines are living patterns cutting through existence like a knife cuts through a multi-layered cake. They are not merely in the visible material world as rivers, mountain ranges, coral reefs or such. They exist in the sky, connecting and traversing the elements, especially the night sky, where they can be seen clearly in the stars. They move in and under the ground under our feet in waterways, cracks, layers and various geological formations. Song-lines slice though our world from top to bottom, from beginning to end. Their patterns remain the same but always different as the world and the universe cycles through their natural changes. This blueprint is the essence of pattern thinking. Standing in the bush, one looks for patterns to discern the flow of water, predominant wind directions and other direct knowledge.

Abdilla explains succinctly what pattern thinking is.

> IKS[101] *syndicates theology, philosophy, science, the arts, ethics and the law through* **Pattern Thinking: being+knowing is interconnection and interrelatedness.** *Pattern Thinking can regulate the delicate balance of all things synthetic and our relationship to them. It is an ethical intelligence and embodiment born from this land, giving meaning and relationship to everything. I take this system, evolved as a streamlined ecology, as the best chance of Australian humanity's maximising its chances of success.*[102]

  209-indigenous-knowledge-systems-and-pattern-thinking-an-expanded-analysis-of-the-first-indigenous-robotics-prototype-workshop/ [Accessed 11 Sep. 2019].
101 Abdilla
102 Angie Abdilla, R. (2019).

Being indigenous and possessing knowledge as a result of being one with the universe leads us to a place of connection and interaction with all things. If we sit with this and allow it to guide how we see the world, we will begin to see the ongoing and ever-changing patterns informing nature.

In contrast, settler and Western thinking rely heavily on definitions and certainty. They need to know and prove what they know. We are comfortable with not knowing and living with uncertainty is key to living in sync with our universe and on country. In a consumer world, people cannot cope with seasons which do not come when they say they should. They cannot do marketing campaigns, run holiday programs, develop seasonal activities without setting in stone – or at least on a printed calendar – when they will begin and end. The uncertainty inherent in Aboriginal thinking is simply not conversant with those who seek to capitalise on nature.

Pattern thinking influenced how my father saw the world, particularly the natural world. In this space, he was at home and comfortable, able to connect the dots, see the lines and make decisions for land and animals which benefited all. Here was a synthesis of the natural, sacred and human world for *"Indigenous philosophy can be seen as comprised by three components, all interlinked and informing the others: Physical World, Human World and Sacred World."*[103]

These three worlds are intertwined and interconnected with no one world holding the supremacy over the other. They are held in balance, not in tension. The task of being Aboriginal is to hold on to each lightly so each balances the other. There is to be no

---

103 Abdilla, R.

tension. Humans are not to seek to use either of the other two for their particular purposes, thus depleting the place they have in our thinking and being. If this occurs, then the whole is out of balance and all will experience the consequences. It is not a competition with winners and losers. It is a metaphysical clasping of hands, the custodial ethic in action on a grand scale.

Abdilla goes on – and my apologies for handing this section over to her – but she does explain it much better than I:

> *Pattern Recognition is a synchronous, intelligent system, a network in which all parts are equal in value, including humanity. It is multi-dimensional and includes the "lifeless", otherwise known as the metaphysic and the cosmic. It is being+knowing at once; epistemology+ontology; complex yet harmonious in its simplicity: it is the Indigenous central nervous system. Repetitiously sung up since time immemorial, the embodiment of Pattern Recognition surpasses knowing and knowledge, and becomes being on a cellular level.*[104]

It is a way of being, embodied by those who participate and are actively engaging in the transfer of knowledge. It ceases to be a philosophical or traditional curiosity and becomes a part of the indigenous knowledge base, available to all who wish to activate it. Abdilla's comment that it surpasses "knowing and knowledge,

---

[104] Angie Abdilla, R., 2019. *FCJ-209 Indigenous Knowledge Systems And Pattern Thinking: An Expanded Analysis Of The First Indigenous Robotics Prototype Workshop*. [online] Twentyeight.fibreculturejournal.org. Available at: <http://twentyeight.fibreculturejournal.org/2017/01/23/fcj-209-indigenous-knowledge-systems-and-pattern-thinking-an-expanded-analysis-of-the-first-indigenous-robotics-prototype-workshop/> [Accessed 11 September 2019].

and becomes being on a cellular level" is essential. It is implicit in the very cells that make up life and make up each human being. We hold within us the wisdom of patterns and, if we listen deeply enough, we can understand life as it resonates with our cells. As we are citizens of the universe, a product of its fecundity, then we can resonate with all sharing these same patterns within, whether they are animate or non-animate, human or non- human. It is why we remain country despite being off or away from home for a long time.

Yunkaporta suggests that you can gather patterns from your environment. If you want to know the patterns of creation, speak to everyone, as everyone carries a part of it no matter how little it may be. "Authentic knowledge processes are easy to verify if you are familiar with that pattern – each part reflects the design of the whole system. If the pattern is present the knowledge is true...."[105]

Everything consists of patterns, and it is always the same pattern, but each is different. It is not static and unchanging. It is dynamic and continuously reinventing itself. You have to remain in dialogue with it to ensure you are in sync with it. In my art practice, I explore what happens when one begins with a straightish line and continues to replicate that line up a large canvas. The line changes and never stops changing. The patterns it creates changes. In some places, they remain all the way through, in others what appeared to be definite and precise change and disappear to be replaced by another pattern, which grows and also goes. The line is the same. Only the pattern has changed.

Pattern thinking speaks to the complexity of indigenous thinking and understanding. Complexity is at the heart of all that

---

[105] Yunkaporta, T. (2019), p. 14.

is within Indigenous Knowledge Systems. It is not simple and unsophisticated and arises out of a sophisticated way of seeing the world. To dismiss it as primitive only speaks to the limitations of the Western imagination's ability to disconnect from duality and superficiality.

WHIN-NGA-RRA

Alongside pattern thinking is anticipation. Being Aboriginal invites you to be anticipatory, to be always looking for what is coming next. Anticipation builds on patterns and looks for the new, the unusual, the unexpected, the not seen before. It engages with the ongoing nature of the dreaming, of creation as a neverending act of which we are a part.

To play our custodial role, we are to be ready for what is next and what we haven't seen before. It is a mindset of possibilities, not one of passive participation. If people are to survive in a hostile environment, they need to be active participants, engaged in an on-going seeing and speaking with the material and the spirit world, the particular and the universal, self and others. Otherwise, the echidnas will take over.

Tyson Yunkaporta reminds us to be careful of echidnas – they may be the next world dynasty – he points out that they have the largest prefrontal cortex relative to body size of any animal. Fifty per cent of their brain is available for thinking big things such as decision-making. Humans? A measly thirty per cent![106]

Anticipation is arguably a creature's most valuable addition to pattern thinking. It keeps us alive. It allows us to address the threats facing us and grasp the opportunities within our world. Echidnas evolved between 20 and 50 million years ago, descending from a platypus-like monotreme. This ancestor was aquatic, but echidnas adapted to life on land. Now that is some time to live an

---

106 Yunkaporta, T. (2019). *Sand Talk*. 1st ed. Melbourne, Vic.: Harper One, p. 1.

anticipatory pattern-filled existence. No wonder they look at us and quickly hide, out of embarrassment.

The 2019-2020 fires destroyed the area around Southern Ocean Lodge on Kangaroo Island, off the coast of South Australia. Fears were held for Enchilada, the resident echidna. When the staff returned, they found him safe and well, wandering along the boardwalk. "Echidnas are well-adapted to Australia's bushfires, having developed the capability to curl into a (spiny) ball and burrow into the ground while the fire passes over them."[107]

Living through extreme heat and ice, covered with water, enduring all the ages of our planet and remaining viable and adaptive in our present period, they probably wonder how we could stuff it all up so quickly! The thirty per cent may play a part!

Our failure as modernists to ignore patterns and anticipation for linear, evidence-based facts, our desire for more and more from less and less has brought us to a stage when we no longer know our home, how it works and what we need to do about it. We are disconnected from the patterns built into the universe, selectively taking only those that fit for us and ignoring those that are necessary for life.

Catastrophic climate events, land degradation and biomass loss all point to our inability to live relative to all else. We cannot see nor hear "The Call of The Reed Warbler"[108], let alone the sound the soil makes as it dies beneath our feet.

---

107 7NEWS.com.au. (2020). *'Little ripper': Resident echidna 'Enchilada' found safe and well on Kangaroo Island*. [online] Available at: https://7news.com.au/lifestyle/good-news/kangaroo-islands-southern-ocean-lodge-finds-resident-echidna-enchilada-alive-and-well-c-647346 [Accessed 21 Jan. 2020].

108 Massy, C. (2018). *Call of the Reed Warbler*. Chelsea Green Publishing.

Whin-nga-rra

Anticipatory people hear and see. Pascoe[109] and Gammage[110] in their groundbreaking books, remind us that you did see but that you ignored what you saw to build a copy of the home you left behind. No wonder the echidnas get a bit spikey about it all.

Whin-nga-rra is a Wiradjuri word meaning to listen, hear and think. It is not just a word describing an idea, but it is an action requiring practice and patience. Whin-nga-rra is integral to anticipation and awareness of what is required and why it is required. It picks up the idea of walking country to hear what it has to say and what you have to do in response. It is deep listening, not with-in but with-out. It is learning to listen to the universe, hear what it is saying to you and to think about how you should and will respond.

Whin-nga-rra is mostly embedded and partly learnt. It comes as software with the hardware at birth. Like all software, one has to learn how to use it to receive the optimum output. Learning to listen involves seeing, hearing, feeling, touching the world around you. It's the downloading of updates for the software. It uses all your senses and your kinship relationships. It is not a solitary sitting and hearing within – that is the last place you go. You go to your big brain, your gut, first, before processing it through your rational brain, your intellect.

As a young boy, I would help my father move sheep with the help of our sheepdog. Dad would remain at the gate, ready to watch as the sheep went through for any issues and to count them to make sure they were all there. You were always mindful

---

109 Pascoe, B. (2014). *Dark emu*. Sydney: Magabala Books.
110 Gammage, B. (2014). *Biggest Estate on Earth*. Sydney: Allen & Unwin.

of moving the sheep slowly for fear of their raising the dust as you walked across the paddock. If a glimmer of dust were visible, he would ask, "Have you got somewhere else to be or do?" If you answered, as we always did, 'No', he would say, "You must have, you raised the dust in your hurry." The dust was evidence you weren't entirely at one with your task, with the sheep or with your self.

It is a challenge for the non-Aboriginal mindset. We are in a hurry to get somewhere else. Whin-nga-rra is a life practice asking for all of our being to be present where we are and what we are doing. It requires us to be aware and conscious of what is happening around us, listening to and reading the patterns, reflecting on what is our responsibility as part of our custodial ethic.

And it takes time, many lifetimes, for this to be embedded in our cellular structure. A Buddhist monk visited the school where I was chaplain. He came from Nepal and was speaking about his experiences. A student asked him how long it had taken him to learn to meditate. His answer shocked the collective mass. He said that it took him six years to learn how to sit and only then did he begin the process of learning how to listen. He didn't say how long that took but intimated it was still going on in his life many years later.

Once you have learnt to listen, you begin to hear, again with all of your being and tradition. You are not to hear your ideas and thoughts, but the voice of the universe, your world or country. It is about understanding the nuances of animal, weather and life behaviour. It is about hearing the patterns and how they are changing or will change so you can then find an appropriate, respectful way to respond.

To think here is not an intellectual act. It is more of a feeling and reflecting response. The action comes after you have reflected on what you have heard and what your gut, tradition and the universe are indicating is the appropriate response. Often there is no action required, merely an awareness so that there are no surprises. What is and will be is ok, and I am ok with that.

Whin-nga-rra allows you to see patterns, hear the songs in the song-line and interpret their meaning for you at this time. It is embedded within our cellular structure and 'birthed' in the processes young boys, and girls engage in before adulthood. These practices enliven this knowledge and anchor it in the community.

Here is a practice integral to Aboriginal ways of seeing. However, the word is different in every Aboriginal language; the way of whin-nga-rra is a common thread through Aboriginal existence.

ALL IN THE SKY

Only a few minutes walk from where my grandmother grew up on the side of a small hill in Wilpinjong; there was a bora ring or burbang, investigated in 1894 by Matthews.[111] It is reasonable to assume that the burbang[112] was known by the Aboriginal people in the Black's camp and those such as the Baileys who lived nearby.

When Matthews surveyed it as part of a study of Bora rings, places of initiation (burbang) and ceremony with an inner and outer ring – the outer ring being for women and the inner ring for the elders and those participating in the ceremony, this ring had similar coordinates to the others studied.[113] They reflected what was in the sky at the time ceremonies such as initiation took place. In this case, it was the position of the emu in the sky.

"What's up there is down here" is a principle, according to Michael Anderson,[114] informing wisdom and practice of Aboriginal culture and ceremony. Michael is speaking relative to Kamilaroi and Euhuahlayi people for whom he is an elder.

It is a principle or way of seeing influencing many other nations and their particular ways of being. The sky and all it reveals provides both practical and ceremonial wisdom people local to a specific area use to define and divine life. Tied in

---

111 Gammage, B. (2014). *Biggest Estate on Earth*. Sydney: Allen & Unwin.
112 Burbang (circle) is a place where a burrbang (initiation) occurs.
113 Jens Korff, C. (2020). *Star Stories of The Dreaming (Film)*. [online] Creative Spirits. Available at: https://www.creativespirits.info/resources/movies/star-stories-of-the-dreaming [Accessed 21 Jan. 2020].
114 Quoted in Michelle Trudgett, (2019). [online] Available at: https://www.academia.edu/34217888/The_emu_sky_knowledge_of_the_Kamilaroi_and_Euahlayi_peoples [Accessed 21 Sep. 2019], p. 8.

with the seasons, patterns of being and the balance of life, the interpretation or responding to the night sky – what we may call Aboriginal astronomy – is integral to Aboriginal people's existence and success.

The emu in the sky is a formation almost universal to Aboriginal people. Some say, when you can see the emu in the sky, you begin to understand Aboriginality. Perhaps this is too simplistic at one level, as there are several formations present but it is one evident in the lore and ceremony of most nations.

In Wiradjuri lore, there are two creator beings with a role in the making of boys into men. We understand Biame made the earth, water, sky, animals, and people. "He makes the rain come down and grass to grow, and welcomes good people to his 'home' in the Milky Way (a place of peace and plenty) on their passing." The identity of the second, Daramulun, a being "whose voice resembles the rumble of distant thunder" is a little less clear. Is he simply another word or form of Biame, perhaps he is a son or maybe just one of Biame's people?

It is traditionally understood boys go with Daramulun and are 'killed' and re-formed by him as men, albeit with one tooth missing. The legend continues in this retelling as follows:

> However, it was apparent that not all of the boys had returned from this ordeal. When questioned by Baiami, the surviving boys reluctantly admitted that Daramulun had not killed and reassembled them, but had extracted their teeth using his own lower incisors. During this process, he sometimes bit off the boy's entire face and then devoured him. In his

> anger on hearing this, Baiami destroyed Daramulun, but put his voice into every tree in the forest. Thus, a bullroarer (Mudthega) fashioned from any tree will have the voice of Daramulun, and hence plays an important role in the Burbung ceremony. Baiami decided not to tell the women and uninitiated about Daramulun's indiscretions, but rather continued to make them believe that boys were still being put to death and restored to life by Daramulun. By doing so, and showing men how to perform tooth avulsion and how the laws were to be passed on, he instituted the first Burbung ceremony, which has been followed by Wiradjuri men ever since.[115]

In this retelling, Daramulun overstepped his mark and earned the wrath and punishment of Biame. All that remains is the sound of his voice hidden in the trees. It is heard when pieces of the trees are transformed into a bullroarer[116] and swung above the head.

It is important to remember there are different tellings of these stories, depending upon where you are. For example, if Daramulun is Baime's son, he may be called Gurra-gala-gali and Baime may be spelt Biyaami. Aboriginal language and lore is mobile in place and use and responds to both stories it tells but loses none of its meaning in either.

---

115 Robert Fuller, *The Astronomy of the Kamilaroi and Euahliya Peoples and their Neighbours*, M.Phil thesis, Macquarie University, accepted 15 March 2014.
116 Several words describe a whirler – dhamaliny, dharramaliyu, bulbul, bububbubumudhiga, mudyigang.

R. S. Fuller writes, "In Aboriginal astronomical traditions, dark spaces within the Milky Way are as significant as bright objects. Two animals symbolically link Bora ceremonies to these dark spaces." These are the Rainbow Serpent and the emu, both traced by dust lanes in the Milky Way.[117] It seems the emu played an essential part of the Burrbung ceremony in the period May to August in southeast Australia. Male emus brood and hatch the emu chicks and rear the young, a responsibility translated into the process involved in the initiation of adolescent boys by their male elders.

Concerning the emu, Yunkaporta tells a story seeming to be at odds with the emu's traditional role, yet it is compatible with the initiation story. The initiation process significantly shifts their focus from themselves as the centre of the world to their role and responsibility in the communal life. It primarily aims to quell the narcissism present and refocus the passion for flourishing community life.

I'll let Tyson tell the story, and you can make up your mind.[118] This is a ...

> Dreaming story of a meeting in which all the species sat down for a yarn to decide which one would be the custodial species for all of creation. Emu made a hell of a mess, running around showing off his speed and claiming his superiority, demanding to be boss and shouting over everyone. You can see the dark shape of the Emu in the Milky Way. Kangaroo (his head

---

117 Fuller
118 Yunkaporta T., *Sand Talk* (1st edition) Melbourne: Harper One 2019, p. 30.

the Southern Cross) is holding him down, Echidna is grasping him from behind, and the great Serpent is coiled around his legs.

Containing the excesses of malignant narcissists is a team effort.

AN INTRICATE WEB OF INTER-BEING-NESS

So what have we found about Aboriginal knowledge systems? The word 'systems' is used with some fear and trepidation as it seems a little too Western, too clinical and mechanistic to describe an equitable relationship way of being that treats all existing in our universe and selves in a hospitable and compassionate manner.

Our lore (law) is not a system as defined by a modern world. It is an intricate web of inter-being-ness hidden in, on and around our land and each particular part thereof. It then looks a little more like a moving jigsaw with each of us being a part, carrying a part of the law within us. If we are to know and transfer knowledge, we must listen to and respect each part of it.

Cold frosty mornings as a child often revealed large-scale spider webs (ganggarrr) hanging between buildings, trees and gate-posts. They were not there the night before, or if they were, they were unseen. This morning, they glisten with the morning dew and catch not only the rising sun but also breakfast and lunch, creatures that fly in and are unable to resist the mesh-like shape the web takes.

Understanding the law (Aboriginality) as a web, we begin to understand the interdependence of being. It is more than a Western-style spirituality. It is actuality in capital letters, real and alive in people and country and all our cousins.

But, wait, there is more. The Traditional Story is courtesy of our ancestors, those who have come before us and wound their way into this highly calibrated way of life. Ancestors are people or at least were people, but they were not only people. They were also non-human beings. Animals and other easy to understand sentient beings, some of which now feature as totems.

Inanimate objects can also be ancestors. For some, rocks, rivers, mountain ranges, trees are here. The Great Dividing Range and its various parts along with Uluru and significant river systems all having been here from the beginning, hold and share knowledge as ancient as they are. Concerning natural disasters, the damage inflicted is more than the physical damage. It is the annihilation of deep spiritual connections and song-lines buried in the ground, carried in flora and fauna and the destruction of trees and the earth.

I was taking part in a conference on spirituality in Alice Springs. We were doing a session on listening and hearing what the landscape was saying. The leader asked us to go outside and find a place to stand still and tune in. I dutiful did so and stood next to a tree, mostly because it was shady. When we went back inside, we were all asked what we heard. When I asked, I explained I was standing next to a tree, and it spoke to me. I waited just long enough to make sure everyone was listening, and I said, "This is it what it said to me, 'Get off my foot, you idiot'".

We need to be careful how we listen for these ancestors do not speak as we do and we have to take the long and arduous task of coming into relationship through the law so that when we are ready, we can hear. You cannot just go out after forty minutes of work-shop and hear. The ancestors, and, come to think of it, our world only responds to a respectful and reciprocal relationship and without that what we may listen to is only our desires echoing back to us.

All around us are smidgens of those who created this place in the beginning. They are not gone, just not fully seen. They are present in each of us and are as minuscule as the very matter that makes us up. It is these smidgens that join us to each other and make us indigenous of the universe. It is from this citizenship that we have the responsibility of care and custodianship along with all others.

Our citizenship takes on many forms, from the particular to the universe and back again. It is circular in motion and moves from one citizenship to another and from one combination of citizenships to others without following a logical straight line. We are citizens of our familial and tribal groups; we are citizens in this modern world of states and countries along with various groups and institutions, and we are citizens of earth and finally citizens of the universe. Our citizenship is stratified, and we can often find ourselves having to balance the requirements of one form in competition with another.

As part of our citizenship, we will find ourselves responsible for various parts of our worlds and, concerning our ancestors, various song-lines or sacred spaces and knowledge. If we think too deeply about this, we can become afraid that we are not enough for the task, especially if separated from country. Remember that our lived culture is the oldest on this planet and that the ancestors go back much further; therefore, they take a long view of life and responsibility. You will be enough when you need to be enough, and you will receive all you need to fulfil your obligations.

Atalanta Lloyd-Haynes reminds us that

> The Law applies to all of us who live on country, whether we believe in it or not: 'Our law is not like whitefella's law. We do not carry it around in a book. It is in the sea. That sea, it knows. Rainbow knows as well. He is still there. His spirit is still watching today for law-breakers. That is why we have to look after that sea and make sure we do the right thing. We now have to make sure whitefellas do the right thing as well. If they disobey that law they get into trouble alright'.
> (Kenneth Jacob, Wellesley Islands, 1997, quoted in Grieves, 2008, p. 371)"[119]

Our law applies to all who are on country regardless of whether they are from country or not as an essential idea. It speaks of the importance of welcome to country and smoking ceremonies and to the importance of acknowledging country.

Acknowledging country is carried out by visiting people from other tribes as a way of saying they accept the law and hospitality of their hosts and will abide by that law while on country.

It often seems appropriate for people to ask Aboriginal people to acknowledge country if it is not suitable for you to do a welcome. I say no. It is incumbent upon gabaas to do the protocol of acknowledgment. By doing so, they acknowledge they are on somebody else's country and have no claim to what

---

[119] Welcometocountry.org. (2019). *A reflection on how western knowledge systems have impacted Indigenous Knowledge systems | Welcome To Country*. [online] Available at: https://www.welcometocountry.org/how-western-knowledge-systems-impacted-indigenous-knowledge-systems/ [Accessed 12 Sep. 2019].

is stolen property. It is a reminder to gabaas that they are on our land not theirs; and need to respect the law of that place in the first instance. Once they do this, they are welcome, but they must do it first, so they become part of the community. They may then find themselves included in a kinship relationship to carry out a conversation, and so others will know where they fit in the community's kinship structure.

Belonging to the community is central to our existence. Unlike the modernist, the individual is not the primary driver of life and satisfaction. That remains with the communal. Our first responsibility lies within our kinship groups, but this is not our only responsibility. All we do in every part of our life is about community, not just a fellow human but about all the world, all we can see and relate to, animate and inanimate. Taking this a step further, as we are all citizens of the universe, everything is united in our extended community. Even gabaas. (Most of the time anyway.)

IN CONCLUSION

My memories of those lazy days in the sun, the chirping birds, the grazing roos and sunbaking goannas all gather at once to join the eastern sunrise and the blazing western sunset that bookend my childhood days. Wandering along behind the milking cows or a mob of sheep and being disturbed by a rearing frill neck lizard or a flock of quails remain present in my memory.

Listening to my father as he painstakingly explained the interconnection of life on the land and how every decision had consequences, was connected, made a pattern and if you did this, then you would need to do that. He would talk about the 'old people' who visited him at night and sat on the end of his bed and talked stuff over. When I asked mum about this, she just smiled and said, "I sleep through it".

He may have had his hopes and dreams dashed, but he remained connected to something denied to him. Grandfather had made my Uncle swear no-one would talk about Grandma's identity. And they didn't and wouldn't and won't. Yet everybody around knew. It is those of us who follow who do, in little bits sometimes, but we do.

Aboriginal life works on circles: kinship circles, seasonal circles (more than four) and life circles, to name a few. These circles hold us even if we don't know it or have not been told about it simply because the blood that courses through our veins. And it won't let go.

My father passed on knowledge and sought for me to gain a 'good' western education so that I could be more than a labourer.

In his life from tree to tree, the one he was born under and the one he died under, he set about making sure we didn't live under the same oppression he felt. He shared knowledge, provided for us to become more and gave me a connection which means I am now on a 'same but different' journey as him – to put right just a little that is wrong, tree to tree. When I die under that second tree, I hope to put something positive in the ground, the repository of sacred knowledge for coming generations.

In *Dark Emu*, Bruce Pascoe quotes W. E. H. Stanner, and it is worth repeating here:

> ...the notion of Aboriginal (Stanner always used a lowercase 'a' for Aboriginal) life as always preoccupied with the risk of starvation, as always a hair's breadth from disaster, is as great a caricature as Hobbe's notion of savage life as "poor, nasty, brutish and short." The best corrective of any such notion is to spend a few nights in an Aboriginal camp, and experience directly the unique joy in life which can be attained by a people of few wants, an otherworldly cast of mind, and a simple scheme of life which so shapes a day that it ends with communal singing and dancing in the firelight .. its principle and its ethos are variations on a single theme – continuity, constancy, balance, symmetry, regularity...[120]

When society sees Aboriginals as people of deficit, needing the Northern Territory Emergency Response (invasion) or the Closing the Gap statistical program to make us the same, or a cash management card to ensure we don't use our money as wealthy white people do, we can despair. We are to remember our Aboriginality or way of seeing. It has held us in good stead for 65,000 years or more and will continue to do so if we trust in it.

---

120 Pascoe, B. (2014). *Dark emu*. Sydney: Magabala Books, p. 139.

This way of life, in sync with the universe, is of the spirit but is not spiritual in Western terms. We do not need the label spirituality. We do not need Christianity.

Our understanding of ourselves in the interlocking world is such that we do not need a saviour or an intervening god. We do not need to give up what has sustained us for millennia simply to go to heaven, a place we never had before colonisation. Yes, there was an understanding of sky places or worlds (murriyang), but they were not places we sought to escape to at the end of our lives, nor were they the places we looked to for salvation. Our culture resolved relationship or kinship problems and the problems of human failings here and now without the need for a sacrifice to set us free. That idea is barbaric to us.

We did not need hell because we did not need duality. There was no good and evil, just what is at the time. Spirits and people cycle together in and out of life moments experienced as just what happens when you are alive. These are live on the continuum between the two trees of life – birth and death. Here our vocation is to live out of the wisdom of country, above, below and here and now. Life is living between the two before becoming one with the dirt of country. At that point, we add to the wisdom and reconciliation inherent in that vocation.

In discussion with a group of cub scouts where I had outlined the journey between trees, one commented that her little brother had lived his life only at the first tree, which was both trees for him. It seemed to give her comfort to understand that life is as long as it needs to be to fulfil our citizenship role. The fact her baby brother had died soon after being born indicated to her that his job was complete. He was now in a place where he continues to contribute to the beauty of the world. It was not a failure of a god, science or medicine. It was as it was, and that is ok.

Now I understand those who practice one of the Abrahamic faiths and who have read this far, may find my assertion we do not need Christianity as practised in a neo-colonial world troubling. It is probably alarming because I am an Anglican priest. It troubles me too, so do not feel special. It should trouble us for several reasons:

- In a world of diversity in every part of our lives, why is there desire that there be only one god and one way to live? Walking through the Australian bush, I recall there are forty species of wallabies, four of kangaroos, seven hundred of eucalypts, six of black cockatoos, one hundred and forty of land snakes and thirty-two species of sea snakes. Why is there but one-way to look at god?

- Why do we need to degrade ways of seeing that are different from ours and which we do not understand? Here is colonialism in another form. If the other does not exist or I cannot imagine it, then it doesn't exist and needs to be eradicated.

- Why is so much of our Abrahamic faiths gender and colour specific and not able to include as equals those who identify differently to us? Colour and gender do not define us. Our humanity and custodial kinship ethic do.

- Why is being spiritual separated from merely being alive and apart of this world, above, below and around us? It is not a separate category. We are spiritual because

In Conclusion

we are indigenous to the universe. It comes with the package and is not a something you add on later.

- Why do we not understand that institutional religion in this country comes from different places with a different language, sets of metaphors and attached to history and a home that is not of here? I have discussed the idea of an Australian Church in my book *Another Time Another Place* which many read as being about Aboriginal people and the church. Because I, an Aboriginal priest, wrote it, it must be. It is not. It is about finding a religion suitable to Australia and all who now live here.

The question that troubles me most personally is why I find myself in this place where I have to hold in tension the two ways of seeing. It would be so much easier to be one or the other. The same goes for my fair skin. It should be black, and life would be more natural, perhaps, maybe. I have come to where I am after a lifetime of not fully knowing and attempting to live out of my whiteness.

My response to those who ask why I do not identify as Irish or English is that for three-quarters of my lived life, I did. I suppressed my Aboriginal heritage and denied its existence. When I spoke about my story for the first time at an event where I was a speaker and attended by elders only, I found myself violently ill, leaving the room to be sick after only a few minutes of my talk. When I returned, they said I would be fine now as I had made peace with the Ancestors and myself. Leaving the room later, one came and said you will do great things for our people now. Tonight is just the beginning.

You cannot avoid who you are.

Now I am finding myself cycling back into my blackness, and it has and is turning my world upside down. I can only imagine God and the Ancestors had a meeting and decided that instead of forcing me to be one or the other they would place me in this situation and see what would happen. They wanted to know how I would resolve it, not so either could boast, but so that I could reconcile within myself who I am.

At times I have been Christian, both evangelical and liberal, and since my mid 40's, I have been living into my Aboriginality. Are these two ideas at odds in my life? No, although I often experience it as yes.

What I have discovered is I no longer assess my Aboriginality through theological perspective. Why? Because if I use doctrinal parametres, I close off my Aboriginality. It is like putting the palm of your hand with the fingers fused in front of your eyes. You only see the hand. You cannot see through it. The givens on which such thinking is predicated prevents you from seeing what is there.

I now look at Christianity through an open hand; the hand is in front of the face, but the fingers are wide apart allowing you to see what is hidden, unlike the previous example. Now I see in the universe what is otherwise unable to be seen because you started at a point of certainty and knowledge.

Through this process, I have added colour, shape and complexity to my Christian worldview by adding it, not as a replacement, but as another lens through which I reflect on my Aboriginal way of seeing. It is not superior or more correct; it is

In Conclusion

no longer the emu of Yunkaporta's story, but another song-line to singing in the ever more complex patterns that make up our lives.

For Aboriginal people, the similarity in diversity was how they understood themselves and others. Small groups of people who recognised their custodial relationship with the land that sustained them and the Traditional Story explaining it did not need to interfere in the understandings and practices of their neighbours. In some ways, their way of seeing was similar, but it was also different, and that was ok. There was no need to conquer others to make them live and believe like us.

Dreams are essential signposts in my discernment of truth and how to live. I see them as places where the spirits can speak and be heard without the noise of everyday life. Before I woke in a panic, I had a dream that said that there is no need for redemption today. It was black but not frighteningly so. Just black and the voice was undeniably indigenous. I never understood what it meant until now.

> We do not need salvation.
> We are spiritual.
> We are enough.
> We are Aboriginal.
> That is all we need to be.

REFERENCES

- 7NEWS.com.au. (2020). *'Little ripper': Resident echidna 'Enchilada' found safe and well on Kangaroo Island.* [online] Available at: https://7news.com.au/lifestyle/good-news/kangaroo-islands-southern-ocean-lodge-finds-resident-echidna-enchilada-alive-and-well-c-647346 [Accessed 21 Jan. 2020].

- Alicespringsnews.com.au. (2019). *CDP work for the dole scheme gets a hammering – Alice Springs News.* [online] Available at: https://www.alicespringsnews.com.au/2017/08/29/cdp-work-for-the-dole-scheme-gets-a-hammering/ [Accessed 12 Sep. 2019].

- AmpeAkelyernemaneMekeMekarle: 'Little Children Are Sacred (2019). .

- Angie Abdilla, R. (2019). *FCJ-209 Indigenous Knowledge Systems and Pattern Thinking: An Expanded Analysis of the First Indigenous Robotics Prototype Workshop.* [online] Twentyeight.fibreculturejournal.org. Available at: http://twentyeight.fibreculturejournal.org/2017/01/23/fcj-209-indigenous-knowledge-systems-and-pattern-thinking-an-expanded-analysis-of-the-first-indigenous-robotics-prototype-workshop/ [Accessed 11 Sep. 2019].

- Anon, (2019). [online] Available at: https://www.academia.edu/34217888/The_emu_sky_knowledge_of_the_Kamilaroi_and_Euahlayi_peoples [Accessed 21 Sep. 2019].

References

- Appiah, A. (2018). *The lies that bind*. London: Profile Books.
- Arabena, K. (2015). *Indigenous to the universe*. Melbourne: Australian Scholarly Publishing, pp. xiii-xiv.
- Archibald, J. (2014). *Indigenous Storywork*. Vancouver: UBC Press.
- Atkinson, J. (2010). *Trauma trails, recreating song lines*. North Melbourne, Vic.: Spinifex Press.
- Bamblett, L., Myers, F. and Rowse, T. (2019). *The difference identity makes*. 1st ed. Canberra: Aboriginal Studies Press, p.47.
- Behrendt, Larissa, in *Decolonising Research: Indigenous Story Work as Methodology*, edited by Jo-Ann Archibald Q'umQ'umXilem, Jenny Bol Jun Lee-Morgan, Jason De Santolo, Zed Books Pty
- Berger, J. and Overton, T. (2017). *Portraits*. London: Verso.
- Boym, S. (2016). *The future of nostalgia*. New York: Basic Books, a member of the Perseus Books Group.
- Brown, L. (2019). *15 Aboriginal Australian Quotes That Will Change Your Perspective On Life*. [online] Ideapod. Available at: https://ideapod.com/10-aboriginal-australian-quotes-will-change-perspective-life/ [Accessed 11 Sep. 2019].
- Bunyan, M. (2019). [online] Artblart.files.wordpress.com. Available at: https://artblart.files.wordpress.com/2013/07/un-settling-aboriginality-dr-marcus-bunyan-july-2013.pdf [Accessed 13 Sep. 2019].

- Carlson, B. (2013). *The politics of identity*. UTS.

- Carthew, M. and Rogers, G. (2007). *Tiddalick the thirsty frog*. London: Collins.

- Climate Change: Vital Signs of the Planet. (2019). *Scientific Consensus: Earth's Climate is Warming*. [online] Available at: https://climate.nasa.gov/scientific-consensus/ [Accessed 20 Sep. 2019].

- Cole-Hawthorne, R., Jones, D. and Low Choy, D. (2019). *An Aboriginal Obligation to Country: Challenging The Status Quo*. [online] Core.ac.uk. Available at: https://core.ac.uk/reader/143900511 [Accessed 12 Sep. 2019].

- Commonground.org.au. (2019). *Connection to Country*. [online] Available at: https://www.commonground.org.au/learn/connection-to-country [Accessed 11 Sep. 2019].

- Dixon, R. (2019). *Australia's Original Languages - An Introduction*. 1st ed. Sydney: Allen & Unwin.

- En.wikipedia.org. (2019). *Cashless Welfare Card*. [online] Available at: https://en.wikipedia.org/wiki/Cashless_Welfare_Card [Accessed 12 Sep. 2019].

- En.wikipedia.org. (2019). *Hans Johannes Hofer*. [online] Available at: https://en.wikipedia.org/wiki/Hans_Johannes_Hofer [Accessed 13 Sep. 2019].

- En.wikipedia.org. (2019). *Jean Starobinski*. [online] Available at: https://en.wikipedia.org/wiki/Jean_Starobinski [Accessed 13 Sep. 2019].

- En.wikipedia.org. (2019). *John L. Bell*. [online] Available at: https://en.wikipedia.org/wiki/John_L._Bell [Accessed 12 Sep. 2019].

References

- En.wikipedia.org. (2019). *Mudgee*. [online] Available at: https://en.wikipedia.org/wiki/Mudgee [Accessed 13 Sep. 2019].

- En.wikipedia.org. (2019). *Stolen Generations*. [online] Available at: https://en.wikipedia.org/wiki/Stolen_Generations [Accessed 13 Sep. 2019].

- En.wikipedia.org. (2019). *Ulan, New South Wales*. [online] Available at: https://en.wikipedia.org/wiki/Ulan,_New_South_Wales [Accessed 12 Sep. 2019].

- En.wikipedia.org. (2020). *Andrew Bolt*. [online] Available at: https://en.wikipedia.org/wiki/Andrew_Bolt [Accessed 11 Jan. 2020].

- En.wikipedia.org. (2020). *Bruce Pascoe*. [online] Available at: https://en.wikipedia.org/wiki/Bruce_Pascoe [Accessed 11 Jan. 2020].

- En.wikipedia.org. (2020). *Peter Dutton*. [online] Available at: https://en.wikipedia.org/wiki/Peter_Dutton [Accessed 11 Jan. 2020].

- En.wikipedia.org. (2020). *Yuin*. [online] Available at: https://en.wikipedia.org/wiki/Yuin [Accessed 11 Jan. 2020].

- Facebook.com. (2019). *Dadirri - A Reflection By Miriam - Rose Ungunmerr- Baumann | Facebook*. [online] Available at: https://www.facebook.com/notes/australian-aboriginal-directory/dadirri-a-reflection-by-miriam-rose-ungunmerr-baumann/10153007928998513/ [Accessed 13 Sep. 2019].

- Fredericks, B. (2019). *'We don't leave our identities at the city limits'* : *Aboriginal and Torres Strait Islander people living in urban localities*. [online] Core.ac.uk. Available at: https://core.ac.uk/reader/16294495 [Accessed 12 Sep. 2019].
- Gammage, B. (2014). *Biggest Estate on Earth*. Sydney: Allen & Unwin.
- Grant, S. (2019). *Australia Day*. Surry Hills, NSW: HarperCollins Australia / RHYW.
- Grant, S., Grant, S. and Rudder, J. (2010). *A new Wiradjuri dictionary*. O'Connor, A.C.T.: Restoration House.
- Griffiths, B. (2019). *Deep Time Dreaming*. Carlton: Black Inc.
- https://www.sbs.com.au/nitv/article/2015/10/22/. (2019). *why-connection-country-so-important-aboriginal-communities*. [online] Available at: https://www.sbs.com.au/nitv/article/2015/10/22/why-connection-country-so-important-aboriginal-communities [Accessed 19 Sep. 2019].
- Jens Korff, C. (2020). *Star Stories of The Dreaming (Film)*. [online] Creative Spirits. Available at: https://www.creativespirits.info/resources/movies/star-stories-of-the-dreaming [Accessed 21 Jan. 2020].
- Johnson, E. (2015). *Ask the beasts*. London: Bloomsbury.
- Kemp, C. and Loughrey, G. (2018). *A Voice in the Wilderness*. Sydney: Anglican Board of Mission - Australia Limited.

References

- Kleinert, S. (2019). *"Jacky Jacky Was a Smart Young Fella": A study of art and Aboriginality in south east Australia 1900-1980*. [online] Openresearch-repository.anu.edu.au. Available at: https://openresearch-repository.anu.edu.au/handle/1885/9239 [Accessed 13 Sep. 2019].

- Langton, M. (2019). *Welcome to Country*. 1st ed. Melbourne: Hardie-Grant Travel, p. 72.

- Lore, N. (2019). *Noongar Lore | Kaartdijin Noongar*. [online] Noongarculture.org.au. Available at: https://www.noongarculture.org.au/noongar-lore/ [Accessed 11 Sep. 2019].

- Loughrey, G. (2019). *Living the Change*.

- Maddison, S. (2008). Indigenous autonomy matters: what's wrong with the Australian government's 'intervention' in Aboriginal communities. *Australian Journal of Human Rights*, 14(1), pp.41-61.

- Massy, C. (2018). *Call of the Reed Warbler*. Chelsea Green Publishing.

- Meacham, S. (2019). *Saga of nude Brett Whiteley's cave painting*. [online] The Sydney Morning Herald. Available at: https://www.smh.com.au/entertainment/art-and-design/saga-of-nude-brett-whiteleys-cave-painting-20090312-gdteuo.html [Accessed 12 Sep. 2019].

- Merriam-webster.com. (2019). *Definition of SPIRIT*. [online] Available at: https://www.merriam-webster.com/dictionary/spirit [Accessed 11 Sep. 2019].

- Merton, T. (1973). *The Asian journal of Thomas Merton*. [New York]: [New Directions Pub. Corp.], p. 296.

- Merton, T. (2002). *The ascent to truth*. San Diego [Calif.]: Harcourt.

- Olson, E. (2018). *And God created wholeness*. 1st ed. Maryknoll: Orbis.

- Pascoe, B. (2014). *Dark emu*. Sydney: Magabala Books.

- Referendumcouncil.org.au. (2020). [online] Available at: https://www.referendumcouncil.org.au/sites/default/files/2017-05/Uluru_Statement_From_The_Heart_0.PDF [Accessed 21 Jan. 2020].

- RegenR8. (2019). *Wiradjuri Dictionary - RegenR8*. [online] Available at: https://regenr8.org/language-revitalisation/apps/wiradjuri-dictionary/ [Accessed 12 Sep. 2019].

- Sarra, C. (2019). *Sambell Oration Dinner 2018*. [online] Available at: https://www.bsl.org.au/events/sambell-oration-dinner-2018/ [Accessed 13 Sep. 2019].

- Schultz, J. (2018). *First things first*. 60th ed. South Brisbane: Martin Betts.

- Songsforteaching.com. (2019). *Dem Bones: Song Lyrics and Sound Clip*. [online] Available at: https://www.songsforteaching.com/folk/dembones.php [Accessed 20 Sep. 2019].

- Stromberg, J. (2020). What is the Anthropocene and Are We In It?.*Smithsonian*, (January 2013).

- Tatz, C. (n.d.). *Genocide in Australia*.

References

- Taylor, P. (2020). AFP eyes case of author Bruce Pascoe's Indigenous Identity. *The Australian*. [online] Available at: https://www.theaustralian.com.au/nation/afp-eyes-case-of-author-bruce-pascoes-indigenous-identity/news-story/b25a51860074332220f35f224df07 2f0 [Accessed 11 Jan. 2020].

- The Conversation. (2019). *Indigenous treaties are meaningless without addressing the issue of sovereignty*. [online] Available at: https://theconversation.com/indigenous-treaties-are-meaningless-without-addressing-the-issue-of-sovereignty-98006 [Accessed 13 Sep. 2019].

- Turner, M., McDonald, B. and Dobson, V. (2010). *Iwenhetyerrtye*. Alice Springs, N.T.: IAD Press.

- W2.vatican.va. (2019). *Laudato si' (24 May 2015) | Francis*. [online] Available at: http://w2.vatican.va/content/francesco/en/encyclicals/documents/papa-francesco_20150524_enciclica-laudato-si.html [Accessed 20 Sep. 2019].

- Welcometocountry.org. (2019). *A reflection on how western knowledge systems have impacted Indigenous Knowledge systems | Welcome To Country*. [online] Available at: https://www.welcometocountry.org/how-western-knowledge-systems-impacted-indigenous-knowledge-systems/ [Accessed 12 Sep. 2019].

- Whiteley. (2019). *Whiteley*. [online] Available at: https://whiteleythefilm.com.au/ [Accessed 12 Sep. 2019].

- Wiradjuriculture.com.au. (2019). *Food – Dhangaang – Wiradjuri Culture*. [online] Available at: https://

wiradjuriculture.com.au/food-dhangaang/ [Accessed 11 Nov. 2019].

- Wiradjuriculture.com.au. (2020). *Food - Dhangaang - Wiradjuri Culture*. [online] Available at: https://wiradjuriculture.com.au/food-dhangaang/ [Accessed 11 Jan. 2020].

- Yunkaporta, T. (2019). *Sand Talk*. 1st ed. Melbourne, Vic.: Harper One.

www.ingramcontent.com/pod-product-compliance
Lightning Source LLC
Chambersburg PA
CBHW072055110526
44590CB00018B/3182